G000123324

REAL CITY

San Francisco

REAL CITY

San Francisco

www.realcity.dk.com

LONDON, NEW YORK,
MELBOURNE, MUNICH AND DELHI
www.dk.com

Contributors
Kristine M. Carber, Peter Cieply, Karen Misuraca, Richard Sterling, Heather Wagner

Photographer
Britta Jaschinski

Reproduced in Singapore by Colourscan
Printed and bound in Singapore by Tien Wah Press

First published in Great Britain in 2007
by Dorling Kindersley Limited
80 Strand, London WC2R 0RL

The information in this Real City guide is checked annually.

This guide is supported by a dedicated website which provides the very latest information for visitors
to San Francisco; please see page 7 for the web address and password. Some information, however,
is liable to change, and the publishers cannot accept responsibility for any consequences arising
from the use of this book, nor for any material on third party websites, and cannot guarantee that
any website address in this book will be a suitable source of travel information.
We value the views and suggestions of our readers very highly. Please write to:
Publisher, DK Eyewitness Travel Guides,
Dorling Kindersley, 80 Strand, London WC2R 0RL, Great Britain.

Contents

The Guide

Real City San Francisco

Stay ahead of the crowd with **Real City San Francisco**, and find the best places to eat, shop, drink, and chill out at a glance.

The guide is divided into four main sections:

Introducing San Francisco – essential background information on the city, including an overview by one of the authors, the top tourist attractions, festivals and seasonal events, and useful travel and practical information.

Listings – eight themed chapters packed with incisive reviews of the best the city has to offer, in every price band and chosen by local experts.

Street Finder – map references in the listings lead you to this section, where you can plan your route and find your way around.

Indexes – the By Area and By Type indexes offer shortcuts to what you are looking for, whether it is a bar in North Beach or a Chinese restaurant.

The Website

www.realcity.dk.com

By purchasing this book you have been granted free access to up-to-the-minute online content about San Francisco for at least 12 months. Click onto **www.realcity.dk.com** for updates, and sign up for a free weekly email with the latest information on what to see and do in San Francisco.

On the website you can:

- **Find the latest news** about San Francisco, including exhibitions, restaurant openings, and music events

- Check what other readers have to say and **add your own comments** and reviews

- **Plan your visit** with a customizable calendar

- See at a glance **what's in and what's not**

- Look up listings by name, by type, and by area, and check the **latest reviews**

- **Link directly** to all the websites in the book, and many more

How to register

> Click on the San Francisco icon on the home page of the website to register or log in.

> Enter the city code given on this page, and follow the instructions given.

> The city code will be valid for a minimum of 12 months from the date you purchased this guide.

city code: **sanfran92783**

introducing san francisco

San Francisco is often called America's most European city. Its natural beauty and cultural savvy are hard to resist, and whether you're looking for a cutting-edge concert or a classy new restaurant, you'll find a world-class example here. Our contributors have selected the best that the city has to offer and we open with the lowdown on what makes it tick.

INTRODUCING SAN FRANCISCO

If San Francisco were a guest at a party, it would wear a cool vintage outfit, bring an impeccable bottle of 1996 Sonoma Cabernet, lay down incredible mixes at the turntables – and then leave the party at its peak to indulge in some further intrigue. With its dizzying views, gaudy Victorian architecture, world-class cuisine, and unpredictable weather, the city is home to those who think, act, and live a little differently, but do it all with a distinctive, ever-evolving style.

Heather Wagner

A Striking Setting

You can't turn a corner in San Francisco without being overwhelmed by beautiful views. There are, of course, the majestic spans of both bridges – the Bay to the east and the iconic Golden Gate to the north – beneath which the rugged Pacific Ocean mingles with the more tranquil waters of the SF Bay. In the vast Golden Gate Park that extends to the ocean, you can wander through a Japanese Tea Garden, take a paddleboat beneath Art Deco bridges, and admire the stunningly modern de Young Museum. Alternatively, take an urban hike from Twin Peaks (Map 10 F5) up to Sutro Tower (Map 10 G4), or from Broadway to the Baker Street Steps to discover the city's beautiful, hidden neighborhood parks and stately mansions. Just remember to wear sneakers; the hills might be pretty, but they can also be tough to climb.

A Wonderful Mix

San Francisco is an incredible hodgepodge of lifestyles, ethnicities, and outlooks. In this compact metropolis technology mavens, counterculture revolutionaries, mixed-media performance artists, biotech engineers, and longshoreman all happily coexist. The city has large African-American, Asian, and Hispanic populations, but you'll also find Russian, Irish, Indian, Lebanese, and Pacific Islander communities throughout its many neighborhoods. Geographically, San Francisco ranges from the staggeringly steep hills of Pacific Heights and Bernal Heights to the broad, flat Richmond and Sunset districts, while architecturally, modern buildings jostle with pre-1906 apartment blocks. And socio-culturally, though über-liberals may outweigh Republican investment bankers, there's a hearty mix of iconoclasts and independent characters who remain blissfully unclassifiable.

West-Coast Bohemian Chic

A laid-back, funky, self-starting spirit infuses all aspects of life in San Francisco. There's an artisan approach to retail with plenty of independent clothing, furniture, record, and book stores; a reliance on seasonal, northern California-grown ingredients in upscale restaurants; and a bar culture that values eclecticism over exclusion. It all

a city primer

adds up to a collective aversion to conformity and a celebration of unique lifestyles that's refreshingly genuine. Local heroes such as Poet Laureate Lawrence Ferlinghetti and celebrated film- and wine-maker Francis Ford Coppola, along with the city's young, charismatic Mayor Gavin Newsom, act as modern – yet maverick – role-models for the population. And while the tie-dyed ghost of the 1960s still haunts parts of Haight-Ashbury, you'll discover that the local style here is far more progressive cool than decaying hippie.

Vibrant Gay Culture

The Castro is located in the heart of the city, bordered by Upper Market Street and the hills of Noe Valley. This neighborhood is a thriving, cohesive gay community, proud home to lively dance clubs, adult novelty boutiques, revivalist theaters, cutting-edge restaurants, and muscle gyms. Demarcated by rainbow flags and other symbols of gay pride, the area attracts visitors and revelers from around the world (sometimes unintentionally: the F Train on Market Street has whisked many unsuspecting Midwestern tourists from Fisherman's Wharf right to the center of the Castro). Sunday nights are especially buzzing, with lines spilling out of The Café *(see p114)* and the Castro Theater *(see p96)*. The attitude of tolerance toward gay, lesbian, bisexual, and transgendered people has a tumultuous yet proud history in the city. During World War II, San Francisco was a point of departure and re-entry for soldiers, and many "dishonorably discharged" gay men decided to remain in the city and build a community. This community has grown, fueling the city's progressive politics, AIDS activism. and sense of open-mindedness. Today, Mayor Newsom's efforts to legalize gay marriage is yet another step in the journey toward GLBT equality.

✅ The Good Value Mark

Cities can be expensive, but if you know where to go you can always discover excellent-value places. We've picked out the best of these in the Restaurants, Shopping, and Hotels chapters and indicated them with the pink Good Value mark.

INTRODUCING SAN FRANCISCO

Some tourists prefer to steer clear of a city's most obvious icons and attractions, but San Francisco's are so linked to its cultural identity that to miss them is unthinkable, if not actually impossible. Some are inextricably part of the city's backdrop, others are almost kitsch in their appeal – but who can really resist a cable-car ride or a hot fudge sundae from Ghirardelli? Here's the shortlist of famous places that give you that "only in San Francisco" feeling.

Golden Gate Bridge

`7 B1`

>> www.goldengatebridge.org • Nos. 29, 43, 82X AC Transit buses

With its soaring towers, painted a vivid "international orange," this bridge was a feat of engineering when it opened in 1937. At 1.7 miles (2.7 km) long it is the third-largest single-span bridge in the world and is an integral part of the city skyline. Walk across it at sunset and watch the city's lights come to life on your way back.

Cable Cars

>> www.sfcablecar.com Run 6am–1am approximately

Only three lines, the remains of a late 19th-century network that was considered an engineering marvel of its time, now carry cable cars that chug up and down the city's steep hills. The California St. Line has few tourists and the Hyde St. Line is a prettier ride than the Mason St. Line. You can hop on anywhere, so avoid the crowded terminus points. **Adm**

Alcatraz

>> www.blueandgoldfleet.com Tours from Pier 41, 9:30–4:30 (to 6:30 in summer)

"The Rock" served as a maximum-security penetentiary from 1934 to 63, with Al Capone among its first official shipment of inmates. It's a little creepy to step inside a cell, even for just a minute, but it's a compelling experience. Be sure to rent the fascinating audio tour, featuring reminiscences of former inmates and guards. Occasional evening tours are less crowded and even more atmospheric. **Adm**

For the very latest on San Francisco go to **>>** www.realcity.dk.com

top attractions

Chinatown `2 E4`
>> www.sanfranciscochinatown.com

The largest community of its kind outside Asia offers a foray into a world still foreign to most Westerners. Aromatic food stalls and incense-scented backstreets compete with souvenir vendors for your attention. Duck into alleyways or stroll along Stockton Street, rather than Grant Avenue, for a more authentic experience *(see p128)*.

Golden Gate Park `11 C4`
>> www.parkssfgov.org • Nos. 21, 29, 38, 71 AC Transit buses

It was once thought impossible to site a park on the "outside lands," covered in scrub and sand dunes as they were. But today this urban oasis, which began to take shape in 1890, boasts two windmills, a lovely conservatory, nine lakes, and plant species imported from every country in the world – except, for some reason, Bolivia *(see pp144–5)*.

Ferry Building Marketplace `2 G4`
The Embarcadero and Market Street • 415 693 0996
>> www.ferrybuildingmarketplace.com Open 10–6 Mon–Sat, 10–5 Sun

Before the Bay Bridge was built in 1936, this stately 1896 structure was a bustling transit hub for ferry passengers. Ferries still dock here, but after a stunning multimillion-dollar refurb in 2003, it's now renowned as a gastronomic center featuring artisanal food producers, cafés, and food-focused shops, and is a popular destination in itself *(see p52)*.

>> *In summer, trips to Alcatraz can sell out a week in advance, so reserve well ahead*

INTRODUCING SAN FRANCISCO

Coit Tower

2 E3

1 Telegraph Hill Boulevard • 415 362 0808 • No. 39 AC Transit bus
Open 10–6 daily

This Art Deco monument crowning Telegraph Hill honors wealthy citizen Lillie Coit (and the city's firemen). It offers superb 360-degree views and overlooks many of the city's famous stairways that are flanked by quaint cottages and private gardens *(see p73)*. **Adm**

Haight-Ashbury

10 G2

>> www.haightstreet.com

In the 1960s, Haight-Ashbury was *the* ultimate hippie destination, and residents included Janis Joplin and The Grateful Dead (who lived at 710 Ashbury St.). Today, the corner of Haight and Ashbury streets boasts a Gap store, and chic boutiques are replacing head shops, but the neighborhood retains a groovy vibe that's rooted in its gritty history.

Asian Art Museum

3 C3

200 Larkin Street • 415 581 3500 • BART Civic Center
>> www.asianart.org Open 10–5 Tue–Sun (to 9 Thu)

Among the city's best-regarded museums, this arguably has the most noteworthy collection. The galleries offer a sampler of art from across Asia, and the setting, in the completely re-imagined former Main Library, is stunning and spacious. Take in, if you can, the bi-monthly Tea Ceremony in the Japanese Tearoom *(see p70)*. **Adm**

top attractions

Lombard Street
1 C3
Cable car to Lombard Street

"The crookedest street in the world" it is not – Vermont is actually San Francisco's most crooked street, but its remote Potrero location isn't as picturesque as Lombard Street's posh Russian Hill setting. Cars line up to ride down the street, and on weekends and in high tourist season this can mean a long wait. To avoid traffic, walk down from Hyde Street.

Fisherman's Wharf
1 C2
>> www.fishermanswharf.org • Cable car to Fisherman's Wharf, Pier 39

For the throngs that continue to flock here each year, the north waterfront's appeal apparently has not been diminished by the influx of tourist traps and T-shirt shops. Despite them, the setting remains as spectacular as ever, with many nice shops and restaurants still to be found, especially around Ghirardelli Square.

de Young Museum
9 C2
50 Hagiwara Tea Garden Dr. • 415 750 3600 • No. 44 AC Transit bus
>> www.thinker.org Open 9:30–5 Tue–Sun (to 8:45 Fri)

With its move into state-of-the art Herzog & de Meuron-designed digs, the de Young has made waves on the city's cultural scene. Its eclectic collections, begun by publishing magnate M. H. de Young in 1895, incline toward the decorative and intricate and focus on art of the Americas, with forays into Africa and Oceania *(see p79)*. **Adm**

>> *You can still see fishermen landing their catch at Fisherman's Wharf if you arrive around 6–7am*

INTRODUCING SAN FRANCISCO

The seasons in San Francisco don't obey conventional rules. The differences between summer and winter can be hard for a visitor to detect – days in December can be dazzling while July can be foggy and feel freezing. That said, spring and summer are generally splendid, with an abundance of outdoor festivals and activites on offer. Just remember the city's cardinal rule: always bring an extra layer of clothing.

Cherry Blossom Festival
www.nccbf.org

For two consecutive weekends the streets of Japantown are taken over by this annual festival celebrating Japanese culture. There's food, artwork, crafts booths, and various activities. The festival begins with a Cherry Blossom Queen pageant and culminates in a parade with floats, dancers, drummers, and the classic Taru Mikoshi, a huge shrine-float carried by some 100 people. **Apr**

SF International Film Festival
www.sffs.org/festival

This 15-day festival attracts high-caliber work and high-profile guests from around the globe. Hundreds of films are screened in theaters around the Bay Area, with a focus on films that don't yet have US distribution. **Apr–May**

Bay to Breakers Race
www.baytobreakers.com

The world's oldest annual footrace was established in 1912 to boost the city's post-quake morale, and has evolved into 7 miles (12 km) of craziness typifying this eccentric city. Many of the nearly 80,000 participants are fun runners dressed in outrageous outfits and in no real hurry to get to the finish line. **Late May**

Carnaval
www.carnavalsf.com

This showy celebration attracts throngs of people to the Mission District for two days of dancing, entertainment, and traditional foods and crafts. The Grand Parade is an extravaganza of spectacular floats, lavish costumes, Brazilian-style samba contingents, international performers, and giant puppets. **Late May**

KFOG KaBoom!
www.kfog.com

The local alt-rock radio station KFOG hosts an annual free afternoon of concerts at Piers 30–32 on the Embarcadero. The day ends with one of America's most spectacular fireworks shows, choreographed to pop and rock music and filling the entire sky above the Bay. **May**

spring and summer

North Beach Festival
www.sfnorthbeach.org/festival

This is the oldest urban street fair in the country, usually attracting upwards of 100,000 people. It reflects North Beach's history as both the city's Little Italy and home of the Beat Generation. The weekend kicks off with the strangely moving Blessing of the Animals at the National Shrine of St. Francis (610 Vallejo St.). Local artisans show a variety of arts and crafts, and restaurants provide gourmet food booths, some with outdoor seating. The main stage at Washington Square Park provides nonstop music, ranging from opera to jazz and blues. **Jun**

LGBT Pride Month and Parade
www.sfpride.org

June is Lesbian, Gay, Bisexual, and Transgender Pride Month worldwide. In San Francisco, events include the SF International Lesbian and Gay Film Festival (www. frameline.org/festival), the SF Pride Run, a Queer Arts Festival, and Pride weekend at the end of the month. Events of the wild weekend begin on Saturday with the Dyke March (www.dykemarch.org), followed by the Pink Saturday party, which fills Castro Street with revelers. The parade on Sunday is the city's largest event of any kind, drawing some 750,000 attendees. **Late Jun**

Stern Grove Festival
www.sterngrove.org

Stern Grove is a lovely natural amphitheater south of the city surrounded by towering redwoods and eucalyptus trees. On summer Sundays, free music and dance events are held here. Events range from classical concerts to world music, pop, and rock gigs. Seating is unreserved, but you can book a picnic table. **Jun–Aug**

Fillmore Jazz Festival
www.fillmorejazzfestival.com

Each Independence Day weekend, 12 blocks of Fillmore Street are cordoned off and turned into the largest jazz festival on the West Coast. The festival features the normal street fair selection of artists, artisans, and food booths, plus several stages of music. **Early Jul**

INTRODUCING SAN FRANCISCO

Fall ushers in the city's hottest, driest days, so many festivals and events take advantage of September and October's baking sunshine and rare warm evenings. The season also brings a wealth of cultural happenings, from the opening galas of the arts organizations to the notoriously naughty Folsom Street Fair. In winter San Francisco quiets down a bit but remains more active than many cities because of its temperate, albeit rainy, climate.

Sausalito Art Festival

www.sausalitoartfestival.org

More than 20,000 pieces of art are exhibited at this outdoor fair, ranging from cutesy to quite interesting, and there are two stages offering entertainment to occupy your attention if you tire of the art. **Early Sep**

San Francisco Blues Festival

www.sfblues.com

The country's longest-running blues festival takes place each year in a spectacular setting on Fort Mason's Great Meadow (Map 8 H1). From Chicago electric-style blues to Memphis R&B, it's all here at this two-day festival, with world-class artists appearing. It's cheaper to buy tickets in advance and there's usually a free Friday concert at Justin Herman Plaza (Map 2 G4). **Late Sep**

Folsom Street Fair

www.folsomstreetfair.org

This huge leather fair usually draws half a million people into its hedonistic embrace, ranging from guys and gals in open-bottomed leather chaps (and nothing else) to drag queens, S&M practitioners, bondage apparatus vendors, and plenty of gawkers. It pretty much takes over the whole SoMa (South of Market) area between 7th and 12th streets and there's something for every fetishist. You just have to see it to believe it. **Late Sep**

Castro Street Fair

www.castrostreetfair.org

The LGBT party calendar kicks off the month with this hugely popular fair, which fills Castro and Market streets with music stages, dance pavilions, food booths, arts and crafts vendors, and lots of eye candy. **Oct**

San Francisco Jazz Festival

www.sfjazz.org

This festival brings an array of top musicians to the city each fall for two weeks or more, with concerts given in venues throughout the city. There are new works by contemporary artists, "Jazz on Film" presentations, dance shows, matinee concerts, and photography exhibits. **Oct**

fall and winter

Halloween Night

Few cities take Halloween as seriously as San Francisco. Revelers dress in creative or frankly outrageous costumes, and congregate along Market and Castro streets, or at the Civic Center plaza (where admission is charged) for food, drink, and entertainment. Be warned: this evening can cause a transit nightmare – forget about getting a cab, and buses around the immediate area can be difficult. MUNI trains are the best bet. **31 Oct**

Dia de los Muertos

www.sfmission.com/dod

The Day of the Dead is an ancient celebration of the continuum of life and death which has been observed for at least 3,000 years in the Americas. In San Francisco, it is influenced mainly by Mexican custom, and includes a procession through the Mission District with marchers dressed as corpses, grim reapers, and skeletons. The parade passes into Garfield Park, which is filled with candle-lit altars dedicated to loved ones who have passed away. **Early Nov**

Chinese New Year

www.chineseparade.com

Celebrations last for more than two weeks after the first new moon of the Chinese New Year and include a flower fair, carnival, footrace, street fair, and the Miss Chinatown USA pageant, culminating in a giant illuminated nighttime parade. Huge crowds come to see the vibrant floats, marching bands, lion dancers, acrobats, and, best of all, the *Gum Lung* at the parade's end, a Golden Dragon of silk, gauze, and velvet, carried by more than 100 martial artists and accompanied by 600,000 exploding firecrackers. **Late Jan/Feb**

Crab Festival

www.onlysf.sfvisitor.org/crab_festival

Dungeness crab season lasts from November until June, but February is festival month. During the festival, crabs are featured on menus all around town, and scheduled activities range from wine-and-crab tastings to crab cruises. Fisherman's Wharf hosts a number of activities, including walking and behind-the-scenes tours. **Feb**

INTRODUCING SAN FRANCISCO

This is one of the easiest cities to reach and to get around in, as long as you keep one thing in mind: traffic. Throughout the Bay Area there are too many people driving too many cars. Fortunately, San Francisco is blessed with a compact design and grid plan that makes it easy to walk, bike, or use public transportation. If you must drive, avoid choke points like bridges and main intersections during commuting hours. For up-to-date traffic information call 511.

Arrival

Swooping in over the Golden Gate Bridge and the vast expanse of the Bay with its many cities glistening on its edges is a sight that inspires even the most jaded traveler. Three international airports serve San Francisco (see below). If you are coming into town by car from Marin County for the first time you may want to surrender the wheel to someone who has done it before – the drive over the Golden Gate Bridge can be awe inspiring.

San Francisco International Airport

Known to locals by its international designation (SFO), this is the largest and busiest of the three regional international airports. This is where most flights from Europe and Asia arrive. Be aware that the entire airport, both the domestic and the international terminals, is non-smoking. It's only 15 miles (24 km) from downtown San Francisco, so it's a quick and easy drive when the traffic is light. During commute hours, though, it can take 45 minutes or more. Taxis and buses are available just outside the terminal, but the easiest way into town is via **BART**. The recently extended track leads right into the international terminal. The ride into town takes about 30 minutes and costs around $5.

All the major car rental companies, such as **Hertz** and **Avis**, have offices at SFO, as well as the other two airports. You'll get the best prices by reserving ahead. At the time of writing, small car rentals start at about $35–45 per day.

Oakland International Airport

Oakland Airport is actually closer to San Francisco than SFO, but it can take a little longer to reach the city, as BART doesn't come to this airport. But there is a regular and frequent shuttle to the Coliseum BART station, which costs about $2 and takes 15–30 minutes depending on traffic. BART from the Coliseum to Powell Street takes about 20 minutes and cost about $3.

Mineta San Jose International Airport

When traffic isn't bad the easiest way to reach San Francisco from San Jose is by car. The 60-mile (96-km) journey takes about 50 minutes. Follow the signs to Highway 101 North; there are no turn offs along the way. Trains to SF depart **Santa Clara Station** several times per day for the 1 hour 40 minute trip, costing about $8. To reach Santa Clara Station take the free **Airport Flyer** (No. 10 bus) from the airport. A taxi to SF would cost around $160.

By Rail

Amtrak's Coast Starlight and California Zephyr trains stop at Emeryville Station, just north of Oakland on the east side of the Bay. Amtrak shuttle buses pick up passengers and take them via the Bay Bridge to a drop point on the Embarcadero near the Ferry Building in San Francisco. From there it's an easy walk to some hotels and a quick taxi ride to others. Embarcadero BART station is just across the street.

Getting Around

While in San Francisco, always remember that the natives call it "the walking city" for a very good reason. As it is only 7 miles (11 km) across it is extremely foot-friendly – most people could easily walk the whole town, given enough time and shoe leather. For routes and schedules of all public transportation see the **Transit Info** website or call 511.

BART

If you need to get around quickly, at least in the southern half of town, the best bet is the Bay Area Rapid Transport rail system. At busy times trains run every 10 minutes, at slower times every 15–20 minutes. It stops running at midnight, except on New Year's Eve. Ticket machines take both cards (credit and debit) and cash.

MUNI

This is the city's system of buses, trolley cars (also known as streetcars), light rail transportation (MUNI Metro), and the famous cable cars. Locals

For the very latest on San Francisco go to ➤➤ www.realcity.dk.com

complain incessantly about the bus service, especially at peak times, but the trolleys and light rail are quite popular. The three lines of the cable cars (California Street, Powell–Mason Street, and Powell–Hyde Street) are the best way to get around in the northeast quadrant. You can flag a cable car down anywhere along their routes (as long as they have an open space) and hop on and pay the $5 flat fare. Or you can buy a Muni Passport for 1, 3, or 7 days of unlimited transportation (priced at $11, $18, and $24 respectively). Either way, you'll avoid the cryptic ticket machines and terribly long lines at stops like Market Street where most tourists board.

Taxis and Other Cars

If you have to get somewhere quickly outside the BART or cable car zones you'll find **taxis** the most convenient mode of transportation. If you're in the center of town, no ride will be more than about 4 miles (6 km) in a straight line. Fares begin at $2.85 and increase $0.45 every fifth of a mile.

If you have a car, a good strategy is to park at a central garage, such as the one under Union Square or the more affordable Sutter-Stockton Garage (at 330 Sutter), then walk or take BART, cable cars, or a taxi. Driving in San Francisco can be vexing.

Other Options

The Ferry Building at the eastern end of Market Street is the place to catch a ferry to the East Bay, Marin County, Angel Island, or Alcatraz. Two companies operate ferries, **Blue & Gold Fleet** and the **Golden Gate Transit**. This is also a good way to tour the Bay (*see p138*). If you work up a thirst, most ferries have bar service.

San Francisco loves bicycles. Except for the crush of downtown this is the perfect city for two-wheeled transportation. Some of the hills are rather steep, but it only feels that way when going up. **Blazing Saddles** is a centrally located bicycle rental shop.

Tours

This being a walking city, it stands to reason that walking tours would be popular and plentiful. One of the most popular is the culinary walking tour of Chinatown given by Shirley Fong-Torres (**www.wokwiz.com**). This tour includes lunch, so costs a modest fee.

Many other tours are conducted by volunteers, especially historical and architectural tours, and cost nothing. The available tours are too numerous to mention, but a good start is at the website of the city's Convention and Visitors Bureau (**www.sfvisitor.org/ visitorinfo/html/walkpdfs.html**).

For a leisurely tour on the water with a drink in hand, sail around the Bay on **Bay Breeze Sailing**'s yacht Glory Days. Two-hour tours begin in Sausalito and include afternoon, sunset, or moonlight cruises. It's advisable to reserve in advance. A more luxurious Bay cruise – and up to Napa Wine Country –that lasts seven days is offered by **American Safari Cruises.** Their small yacht tours offer great food and wine, as well as wonderful people to show you the best of the Bay.

Directory

Airport Flyer
408 321 2300 • www.vta.org/
schedules/SC_10.html

American Safari Cruises
888 862 8881 • www.amsafari.com

Amtrak
800 872 7245 • www.amtrak.com

Avis
800 831 2847 • www.avis.com

BART
510 465 2278 • www.bart.gov

Bay Breeze Sailing & Yacht Charter
415 381 2760 • www.sailsfbay.com

Blazing Saddles
415 202 8888
www.blazingsaddles.com

Blue & Gold Fleet
415 705 5555
www.blueandgoldfleet.com

Golden Gate Transit Ferries
415 923 2000
www.goldengateferry.org

Hertz
800 654 3131 • www.hertz.com

Mineta San Jose International Airport
408 501 7600 • www.sjc.org

MUNI
415 673 6864 • www.sfmuni.com

Oakland International Airport
510 563 3300
www.oaklandairport.com

SF International Airport
650 821 8211 • www.flysfo.com

Santa Clara Station
www.acerail.com

Taxis
DeSoto Cab 415 970 1300
Yellow Cab 415 626 2345

Transit Info
511 • www.transitinfo.org

⟩⟩ *The best place to hail a taxi is outside a major hotel such as the Westin St. Francis* (see p153)

Making the most of your journey depends to a great extent on having the basic information about your destination: where to get your cash, how to connect with the folks at home, or even where to find a public restroom. Remember that San Francisco is a most welcoming city – the locals will always be ready to help you on your way.

Disabled Organizations

Disabled services and information are available from the **Independent Living Resources Center of San Francisco,** which has its offices in the SoMa district. One of the best sources of information on wheelchair accessibility and other needs of disabled travelers is the website of Access Northern California (**www.accessnca.com/san_francisco**). NB: At the time of writing they have not updated to reflect that BART now comes right into the international terminal of SFO.

All BART trains and stations are wheelchair-accessible, as are all MUNI stations. The Street and Transit Map published by MUNI indicates which routes are wheelchair friendly. For travel information, *see pp182–3.* The major car rental companies can usually provide hand-operated vehicles if given advance notice.

While San Francisco is very friendly to disabled travelers, Berkeley is even more so. For the visually impaired, the traffic lights at major intersections emit a chirping sound to indicate when it is safe to cross. **The Center for Independent Living** can provide up-to-date information and advice. One of the most interesting developments is **Wheelchairs of Berkeley,** an outfit dedicated to the design of leading-edge wheelchairs, which has branches in both Berkeley and San Francisco.

Emergencies and Health

If you witness or fall victim to a crime, call **911**. If you are robbed you will need to file a police report in order to make use of your travel insurance. The most common run-in that travelers have with the police arises from drinking alcohol in the street – many sidewalk pubs and restaurants spill out on to the streets but drinking on the street is illegal.

For a medical emergency the best thing is to head to **San Francisco General Hospital**. The 24-hour emergency services are first rate. You won't have to fill out forms or show proof of insurance, though you would if you were to make an appointment. For non life-threatening situations you might consider the famous **Haight Ashbury Free Clinic**. Services are by appointment only, but there is no charge levied. **Walgreens** drugstore on Powell Street is a good, central pharmacy, and **Western Dental Centers** is a dental clinic near the Civic Center.

Gay and Lesbian Travelers

This being San Francisco it hardly needs to be said that there is a vibrant, and very visible, gay community here. For information and advice you might like to visit the **Lesbian Gay Bisexual Transgender Community Center**. The city's biggest gay party is the annual parade at the end of Gay Pride month (**www.sfpride.org**) in June *(see p17)*.

Listings/What's On

There are three free tabloids, published weekly and seen at virtually every newsstand in the Bay Area, which are good sources of local event listings. These are the *San Francisco Bay Guardian* (**www.sfbg.com**), SF Weekly (**www.sfweekly.com**), and the *East Bay Express* (**www.eastbayexpress.com**). The best-known print source of weekly goings-on across the board is the Sunday edition "Pink Section" of the *San Francisco Chronicle* (**www.sfgate.com**). Online sources are abundant and include the website of the Convention and Visitors Bureau, **www.sfvisitor.org**. Good sites for experimental art and events are **www.fecalface.com** and **www.sfstation.com**. Also check out **www.sanfrancisco.citysearch.com**.

Money

Most methods of payment will find acceptance somewhere in town, though you could have a problem with personal checks. A credit or debit card is usually needed for hotel reservations, and nowadays certain high-end restaurants require a credit card number to secure a reservation. If you should cancel without due notice you'll be charged a penalty.

Traveler's checks (in US dollars) are good almost anywhere, even tow companies, and most restaurants and bars. Foreign currency can be exchanged at banks and foreign debit cards are usually accepted by local ATMs. PIN technology is used in shops, gas stations, and even some bars, but it is not yet commonly used in restaurants.

Opening Hours

Most small and family-run **shops** open between 9am and 10am and close between 5pm and 6pm. Department, record, and clothes stores will close as late as 9pm or 10pm. Most shops are open 7 days a week, while **museums** and **galleries** will often close one day a week, often Monday.

Opening times for **restaurants** vary with type, size, and location. Prominent restaurants are usually open daily for lunch and dinner, closing between 9pm and 10pm, but in Oakland and Berkeley they tend to be closed on Mondays. Most **bars** are open from about 11am. Last call is announced at 1:30am and empty glasses are collected at 1:45am, with doors closing promptly at 2am.

Phones and Communications

Internet cafés seem to be almost as common as fast food outlets. They are especially plentiful in the Financial District and the Mission. **Café.com** at 120 Mason Street is said to have the fastest connectivity in town. Virtually all hotels catering to business travelers, and many simpler hostelries, will have in-room Internet access. If you carry a laptop with WiFi capability you can find a spot by consulting **wififreespot. com/ca.html**. An increasing number of coffeehouses are offering free WiFi. Local calls from public payphones cost $0.50.

Sales Tax

An 8.5% sales tax is added to everything you buy. You can expect a 14% tax on hotel accommodation.

Security and ID

Security is tightest in government buildings, ferry landings, and airports. BART has closed all its public restrooms until further notice. The Bay View and Hunters Point areas, in the southeast of the city, are places to avoid at night.

You should always carry photo ID, especially if you look under 35 and want to enter a club. Be aware that you must have your driver's license with you to operate any motor vehicle.

Tipping

The standard 15% minimum applies to restaurant meals. Calculate that from the pre-tax amount – you are not expected to tip on the tax. Coat check staff receive $1 per garment and bartenders and cocktail servers $1 per drink. For taxi drivers $2–3 dollars is fair, and you'd usually give the same for valet parkers. Hotel bell hops and airport skycaps get $1–2 per bag, depending on size and weight.

Tourist Information

The helpful staff at the **San Francisco Visitor Information Center** can answer most questions. They also provide a range of brochures and maps, and maintain an information hotline *(see Directory)*. Open 8:30–5 Mon–Fri.

Washroom Facilities

Almost uniquely among American cities, San Francisco has a number of convenient, self-cleaning public toilets. They're about the size of a minibus, painted forest green, and they only cost $0.25 to use. For a map, see **www. sfgov.org/site/sfdpw**.

Directory

The Center for Independent Living
2539 Telegraph Ave., Berkeley
510 841 4776 • www.cilberkeley.org

Directory Enquiries
411

Emergencies
911

Government Info & Services
311 (non-emergencies)

Haight Ashbury Free Clinic
558 Clayton St.• 415 487 5632

Independent Living Resources Center of San Francisco
649 Mission St. • 415 543 6222

Lesbian Gay Bisexual Transgender Community Center
1800 Market St. • 415 865 5555
www.sfcenter.org

National Organization on Disability
www.nod.org

San Francisco General Hospital
1001 Potrero Ave. • 415 206 8000

San Francisco Public Library
100 Larkin St. • 415 557 4400
www.sfpl.org

San Francisco Visitor Information Center
900 Market St. • 415 391 2000
www.sfvisitor.org

Walgreens
135 Powell St. • 415 391 4433
www.walgreens.com

Western Dental Centers
1282 Market St.
415 552 1200
www.westerndental.com

Wheelchairs of Berkeley
2911 Shattuck Ave., near Ashby Ave.
510 549 8727
590 Howard St.
415 284 9424

restaurants

The Bay Area restaurant scene has for years been recognized as one of the world's most influential, and the careers of celebrity chefs are followed here like those of sports stars. San Francisco's restaurants are best known for their emphasis on a rich supply of locally sourced foods, and there's also a great variety of venues – from burrito shacks to five-star destinations. The latest trend is clubby, DJ-driven dining lounges.

RESTAURANTS

Ten years ago, dot.com-boom madness informed the city's dining ethos. A restaurant had to be Impressive, a temple to food, offering artisanal products and pristine presentations. Thankfully, those days have gone and we can finally have some fun. Boutique purveyors still supply most restaurants, but there's a new party spirit that's palpable, not only in the whimsy of some chefs' creations but also in a fresh focus on atmosphere in dining spaces.

Peter Cieply

Hot Spots

Good things come to those who wait, so reserve well ahead for these popular destinations. Foodies flock to **A16** *(see p36)*, a chic trattoria serving rustic cuisine from Campania. At **Myth** *(see p30)*, the Cal-French food is as superb as the room is stylish, while fusion **Levende Lounge** *(see p43)* becomes a DJ-driven lounge after dining hours.

Dining Destinations

If you haven't reserved, try strolling these streets to find dinner-on-the-spot. The gritty Valencia Street corridor in the Mission district is dotted with great eateries, from burrito stands to French cafés. Cow Hollow's Chestnut Street is a more yuppified hub, while East Bay's College Avenue has a laid-back feel and plenty of great dining options.

Innovative Menus

When it works, daring cuisine offers a thrilling sensory experience. At super-stylish **Frisson** *(see p31)*, garnishes like foams and scented oils are often used, while **Restaurant Michael Mina's** *(see p29)* artful preparations perfectly suit its modern decor. Relative newcomer **Ame** *(see p41)*, with its Asian-Italian menu pairings, has the city buzzing.

choice eats

Romantic Dining Rooms

For a memorable night out with someone special, head to **Fleur de Lys** *(see p32)*, often called the city's most romantic room. Champagne is *de rigeur* at the lavishly decorated loft that's home to upscale **Jardinière** *(see p38)*. The more humble **Café Jacqueline** *(see p33)* is a picture of sweet simplicity, and serves only soufflés, meant to be eaten *à deux*.

The Great Outdoors

When the weather calls for alfresco dining, it's hard to beat the romance of **Foreign Cinema** *(see p44)*, where films are screened in the dining courtyard. Downtown, **Café Claude** *(see p29)* is a perfect bistro located in a charming alleyway; but for great vistas, visit **Sam's Anchor Café** *(see p47)*, where you dine on a huge deck with city skyline views.

Around the World

This multiethnic city is known for its cosmopolitan cuisine. The tasty dim sum at **Yank Sing** *(see p40)* are a must-try, while fish-lovers should reserve a table at the exquisite **Sushi Ran** *(see p47)*. Moroccan food draws hip, happy diners to **Baraka** *(see p43)*, and **Kokkari Estiatorio** *(see p30)* serves refined Greek food in a spectacular setting.

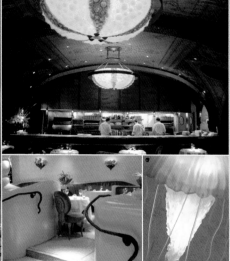

Farallon *undersea fantasy* `3 D1`

450 Post Street • 415 956 6969

>> www.farallonrestaurant.com Open dinner nightly

San Francisco has plenty of crab shacks and fish houses if you're simply looking to satisfy a seafood craving, but none of them makes a splash like Farallon. Named for the rocky, windswept islands off the city's coast, Farallon's fantastic undersea decor and sophisticated, fish-of-the-world cuisine make it an incomparable dining experience.

The restaurant is housed in an historic and architecturally important 1924 building. Diners are received in the "jelly bar," which is lined with octopus-style stools and columns of kelp, and lit by hand-blown glass jellyfish chandeliers. A sandy-looking path leads to the sweeping "caviar" staircase, the surface of which is encrusted with 50,000 cobalt-blue marbles. The Nautilus Room contains six circular booths grouped around a spiraling pillar, while the cavernous Pool Room features mosaic paintings of bathing beauties and sea-urchin light fixtures on the arched ceilings. The original indoor swimming pool from which the room derives its name is still in use below the restaurant. The giddy marine motif extends to the smallest details, such as the swirling velvet upholstery and copper "scales" on the kitchen range hood.

Fortunately, Farallon is not all show. Chef Mark Franz, who spent years as the executive chef of the city's renowned but now-defunct Stars restaurant, creates dishes that more than live up to the surroundings. His "coastal cuisine" features innovative preparations of fresh fish and seafood from near and far, often featuring rarities such as Santa Barbara sea urchin and other unfamiliar species. You might start with Maine scallops and Manila clams and move on to seared English turbot, black cod with a bone-marrow crust, Hawaiian *hebi* (spearfish) with Dungeness crab risotto, or steamed salmon and wild striped bass with shellfish mousse and foie gras sauce. The cooking sounds opulent, and it is, but it's also simple, artfully showcasing the fresh flavors of the sea. The full dinner menu is also served in the bar. **Expensive**

Café Claude *a slice of Parisian living* `2 E5`

7 Claude Lane • 415 392 3505
>> www.cafeclaude.com
Open lunch & dinner Mon–Sat, dinner only Sun

With its French café furnishings and cool clientele, this alleyway bistro is a Parisian haven in the heart of downtown. The food is simple and delicious, ranging from standards (*salade Niçoise, croque monsieur*) to the less expected (salmon in beet *nage*). **Cheap**

Restaurant Michael Mina *fine dining* `4 E1`

Westin St. Francis Hotel, 335 Powell Street • 415 397 9222
>> www.michaelmina.net Open dinner nightly

This refined restaurant makes fine dining feel new. The lofty hotel lobby setting has had an elegantly contemporary update with muted-color fabrics and carpeting. Each course is presented as a trio – a single ingredient prepared three ways – but it all manages to feel unfussy while being truly fabulous. **Expensive**

Cortez Restaurant & Bar *small plates* `3 D1`

Hotel Adagio, 550 Geary Street • 415 292 6360
>> www.cortezrestaurant.com Open dinner nightly

Cool crowds throng this narrow restaurant and bar serving Mediterranean-fusion small plates. Its interior is a stylish mix of Mondrian color panels, chandeliers, mahogany wood, and cork-covered columns.

Chefs Louis Maldonado and Seth Bowden turn out intricate delicacies, such as *katafi*-crusted crab cakes with tarragon aioli. But they're also great at keeping things simple: a striking tarragon-pea foam tops "shots" of fresh spring onion soup; marinated tuna crudo is served on a bed of fennel together with herbs and shallot oil. Dishes are slightly larger than average for "small plates" but you'll still need several to make a filling meal. The dishes are meant for sharing, but you'll invariably wish you'd kept more to yourself. Save room for the *beignets* with chocolate fondue, a heavenly take on *churros con chocolate*. **Cheap**

Cheap: up to $18 for a main course; moderate: $19–29; expensive: over $29

Restaurants

Kokkari Estiatorio *food fit for the gods* `2 F4`
200 Jackson Street • 415 981 0983
» www.kokkari.com
Open lunch & dinner Mon–Fri, dinner only Sat

This Jackson Square restaurant calls itself a "taverna," but Greek food has rarely been so refined, or its setting so gracious. Five million dollars went into creating this take on a Mediterranean country inn, and it shows. Rough-hewn, recycled barn wood forms the framework, and rich accents like fine rugs and oilskin lampshades create a warm, inviting ambience throughout the series of rooms. The food is similarly elegant. The owners set out to elevate Greek food, to have it taken as seriously as other European cuisines, and they have succeeded brilliantly. The moussaka is fragrant, lightened with a yogurt béchamel; cinnamon-scented lamb shank melts off the bone; roast bass is tender and delicious, and, unlike at a typical taverna, they bone it in the kitchen. The lemony oven-roasted potatoes are simply to die for. **Moderate**

Rubicon *fine food with great wines* `2 F4`
558 Sacramento Street • 415 434 4100
» www.sfrubicon.com Open dinner Mon–Sat, lunch Wed

This lauded, classic downtown spot is a favorite of business diners, and a smart splurge for the rest of us. The Cal-Fusion menu is adventurous and the fantastic wine list – some 1,600 selections on the list and 17,000 bottles in the cellar – can match any dish or satisfy almost any vinous desire. **Expensive**

Myth *cool Cal-French cuisine* `2 E4`
470 Pacific Avenue • 415 677 8986
» www.mythsf.com Open dinner Tue–Sat

Myth is an understandably popular spot, offering good food in a sleek but relaxed environment. Sean O'Brien, a protégé of celebrity chef Gary Danko, serves sophisticated comfort food, like prawn and fennel pizzas, and braised beef cheeks. The large bar area (where the full menu is also available) is chic and lively. **Moderate**

Frisson *smart and stylish scene*

2 F4

244 Jackson Street • 415 956 3004
≫ www.frissonsf.com Open lunch & dinner Mon–Fri, dinner only Sat & Sun; bar open to 2am

A clubby dining lounge which has certainly added a *frisson* to the newly hot Jackson Square area. The intellectual New American cooking perfectly suits the futuristic decor in this stylish DJ-driven room. The central, circular dining area is topped with a dome dotted with rings of lights that slowly change color, making it look like a spaceship coming in to land. Seating is on banquettes, upholstered pods, and Eero Saarinen chairs. Above the bar, a back-lit photomural of champagne bubbles has an eerie beauty. In short, this place is cool. The small- and large-plate menu features inventive and exquisite dishes flavored with local seasonal ingredients, but the emphasis of the experience seems to be on the scene. Service can be almost deliberately slow, so enjoy the drinks and the atmosphere. **Moderate**

Bocadillos *trendy tapas bar*

2 E4

710 Montgomery Street • 415 982 2622
≫ www.bocasf.com Open breakfast, lunch, & dinner Mon–Fri, dinner only Sat

This Basque-influenced tapas and *bocadillo* (sandwich) spot is a stylish gem. Don't pass up the foie gras roll with serrano ham, mango, and balsamic vinegar – it's unbelievable. There are no reservations, so go early or squeeze in with the happy crowd. **Cheap**

Bix *swank hideaway with great food*

2F4

56 Gold Street • 415 433 6300
≫ www.bixrestaurant.com Open dinner nightly & lunch Fri

A former Barbary Coast gold-weighing house is now home to a supper club with the feel of a 1940s ocean liner. The food is upscale American – seared tuna with chanterelle mushrooms, chicken hash – and live jazz is featured nightly. Happy hours are popular with creative types and Financial District honchos. **Expensive**

Restaurants

The Slanted Door *elegant Vietnamese* `2 G4`
1 Ferry Building • 415 861 8032
>> www.slanteddoor.com Open lunch & dinner daily

Chef Charles Phan's gleaming new restaurant is already legendary. It's as frequently mentioned in the *New York Times* as it is locally, and visitors and natives alike vie for white-hot reservations.

The enormous waterfront room is ultrasleek, with floor-to-ceiling windows looking out onto the Bay. If it feels a little like an airport lounge, details like the sculptural wall of stacked aqua-colored glass separating the kitchen from the dining room and the striking artworks on the walls give it pizzazz.

The food focuses on simple Vietnamese preparations of local, mostly organic, ingredients, and everything is house-made, down to the fish sauce. So although you'll find traditional shaking beef (a house specialty), spring rolls, and papaya salad on the menu, you'll also find Dungeness crab with cellophane noodles or scallops with organic spinach. **Moderate**

Fine Dining and French Cuisine

Despite San Francisco's reputation as a cutting-edge gastronomic hot house, the most celebrated of its high-end fine dining establishments are all French. The good news is, they each have a stellar chef at the helm giving the cuisine a signature spin.

At **Aqua** (Map 2 F4, 252 California St., 415 956 9662, www.aqua-sf.com), chef Laurent Manrique focuses on the freshest fish and seafood in a sleek and showy downtown dining room filled with dappled lighting and towering flower arrangements. The bar is also a surprisingly popular after-work destination.

Melissa Perello at **Fifth Floor** (Map 4 E2, Hotel Palomar, 12 Fourth St., 415 348 1555, www. fifthfloorrestaurant.com) offers elaborate and exquisitely prepared creations served in a lush lounge setting with zebra-stripe carpets. Under chef Hubert Keller, **Fleur de Lys** (Map 3 D1, 777 Sutter St., 415 673 7779, www.fleurdelyssf.com) is perhaps the most old-fashioned of the bunch, offering simple, elegant French fare in a luxurious dining room that many regard as the city's most romantic.

Chef Gary Danko's five-star restaurant, **Gary Danko** (Map 1 B2, 800 North Point, 415 749 2060, www. garydanko.com), is a showcase for his classical preparations of locally grown foods, inflected with Mediterranean and regional American accents. The dramatic dining room exudes a sophisticated mix of California cool and Manhattan chic. **Masa's** (Map 2 E5, 648 Bush St., 415 989 7154, www. masasrestaurant.com) is a glamorous setting for chef Gregory Short's "New French" food, with modern art, and oversize-lampshade chandeliers. The tasting menus offer exquisite and artful combinations. Former Masa's chef Ron Siegel is now at the five-star **Ritz Dining Room** at the Ritz-Carlton (*see p152*). His cooking adds panache into the otherwise august Old World dining experience.

Tablespoon *modish nightspot*   `1 B4`
2209 Polk Street • 415 268 0140
>> www.tablespoonsf.com   Open dinner nightly

Trendy locals gather in this genial setting for seasonal New American food. On the menu is the typical macaroni and cheese, but also dishes like wild salmon tartare and smoked sturgeon pizza. The wine list is cheeky and easy-to-use: the champagne category is simply called "Bling! Bling!" **Moderate**

Hyde Street Seafood House & Raw Bar *classic fish and seafood*   `1 C4`
1509 Hyde Street • 415 931 3474
>> www.restaurant.com/hydestreetca   Open dinner nightly

A cozy, neighborhood fish house with fresh food at reasonable prices. This Russian Hill charmer's menu goes beyond the basics, specializing in delicious, moist fish en *papillotte* (baked in parchment). The raw bar is a great deal, especially at happy hour. **Moderate**

Café Jacqueline *stellar soufflés*   `2 E3`
1454 Grant Avenue • 415 981 5565
Open dinner Wed–Sun

Jacqueline Margulis has been singlehandedly whisking up soufflés in this romantic little North Beach storefront for more than two decades, and they are heavenly. Aside from a few appetizers, soufflés are the only thing on offer, and they're meant for sharing so if you don't have a love interest, find one. **Moderate**

Pesce *Venetian small plates*   `1 B4`
2227 Polk Street • 415 928 8025
Open dinner nightly, brunch Sat & Sun

Seafood *cicchetti* (small plates) and other Venetian dishes star at this sophisticated Polk Gulch district seafood bar. Don't miss the braised octopus salad, squid ink risotto, or Sicilian swordfish rolls. Great specialty cocktails include the Venetian (gin and orange moscato) and a blood-orange margarita. **Moderate**

Restaurants

Greens *Zen vegetarian classic* `1 A2`
Bldg. A, Fort Mason Center, Marina Blvd. • 415 771 6222
» www.greensrestaurant.com
Open lunch & dinner Tue–Sat, dinner only Mon, brunch Sun

This vegetarian restaurant is set in a spacious converted warehouse, with high ceilings and a wall of windows looking straight out at the Bay and the Golden Gate Bridge. The room was built by carpenters from the San Francisco Zen Center *(see p141)*, and the restaurant is supplied in part by Green Gulch Farm, a Buddhist collective about an hour north of San Francisco. Chef Annie Somerville oversees daily-changing menus that rely on the freshest organic produce. Presentations have as much visual as gastronomic appeal, and while rosters of ingredients can sound complicated they end up harmonizing transcendently. Even a simple "garden salad" is described as "romaine and tat soi with Manila mangoes, papaya, kumquats, pistachios, and citrus chili vinaigrette." If you're picnicking, Greens To Go offers terrific takeout. **Cheap**

A16 *chic Campania cooking* `8 G2`
2355 Chestnut Street • 415 771 2216
» www.a16sf.com Open dinner nightly, lunch Wed–Fri

Foodies flock to this chic Marina District trattoria for rustic cuisine from Campania and truly authentic thin-crust pizzas – chef Christophe Hille is one of only a few certified *pizzaiolos* in the US. As good as the pizzas are, don't fill up, because the rest of the menu is glorious, offering simple, rustic preparations of the freshest ingredients. For starters, try the house-made fresh *burrata* cheese, oozingly creamy and delicious, and drizzled with artisinal olive oil. Pastas are similarly distinctive, featuring uncommon noodle types topped with simple, delicious sauces, like *maccheronara* with tomato ragu and riccota salata cheese. Main dishes might include roasted lamb riblets served with lamb sausages and rocket leaves, or pork breast braised with peppers and olives. The Italian and New World wine list is extensive and the desserts are well worth saving room for. Reservations are a must. **Moderate**

Gourmet Carousel *cheap Chinese* 1 B5
1559 Franklin Street • 415 771 2044
Open lunch & dinner daily

This nondescript-looking but terrific family restaurant in Pacific Heights is always packed with Asians, a good barometer for judging Chinese restaurants. The garlicky pea sprouts are not to be missed. Be prepared for crowds and brusque service as the evening progresses. They also do a brisk takeout business. **Cheap**

La Méditerranée *amazing meze* 8 H4
2210 Fillmore Street • 415 921 2956
>> www.cafelamed.com Open lunch & dinner daily

You need to know only two words: Mediterranean meze. Order this to share and they will literally cover your table with tasty Armenian-Mediterranean treats, including creamy hummus, flaky filo-wrapped spinach and feta, and succulent pomegranate chicken – all for an unbelievably low price. **Cheap**

Quince *elegantly cozy Italian* 3 A1
1701 Octavia Street • 415 775 8500
>> www.quincerestaurant.com Open dinner nightly

Chef Michael Tusk's Chez Panisse *(see p46)* credentials show in the care he takes with fresh ingredients, and his simple preparations of rustic Italian fare have won rave reviews. The room's bisque walls, creamy Murano glass chandeliers, and burgundy banquettes make a lovely setting. **Moderate**

Balboa Café *clubby Cow Hollow institution* 8 H2
3199 Fillmore Street • 415 921 3944
>> www.plumpjack.com
Open lunch & dinner daily, brunch Sat & Sun

Known locally as a hot spot for yuppies on the prowl, this 1913 saloon is also a first-rate restaurant, great for burgers and steaks but just as adept at risotto or grilled salmon. Famous for its brunches, this is a great place for Bloody Marys with the ball game. **Moderate**

Nectar Wine Lounge *chic light bites* 8 G2
3330 Steiner Street • 415 345 1377
>> www.nectarwinelounge.com Open dinner Mon–Sat

It's tough to get into stylish, tiny, no-reservations Nectar, but it's worth the wait. More than 40 world wines by the glass and 800 by the bottle are offered, along with imaginative small plates like bacon-wrapped seared scallops or crispy shrimp tacos. Wine tasting "flights" change weekly. **Moderate**

 Clement Street (see p129) in the Richmond district is a second Chinatown, with many Asian restaurants

Jardinière *dinner with drama* `3 B3`

300 Grove Street • 415 861 5555

>> www.jardiniere.com Open dinner nightly

This luxe loft conversion across from the Opera House might more aptly be named "Champagnoise." The swank decor takes champagne as a central theme, from the lighted glass-and-pewter icebuckets on the swooping balcony rails to the lovely domed ceiling set with tiny sparkling lights. The room is romantic, almost camp in its drama, and a jazz trio plays nightly in the open balcony, adding to the festivity.

The cooking is just as splendid, if less flamboyant. A daily-changing Cal-French menu features seasonal ingredients – many of them organic and from local artisanal producers – and sustainably harvested fish and seafood. You might start with a pork rillette terrine, then move on to wild king salmon with apple cider-grain mustard beurre blanc sauce. Naturally, the champagne and wine lists are extensive, including many choices by the glass. **Expensive**

RNM Restaurant *hip, upscale simplicity* `10 H2`

598 Haight Street • 415 551 7900

>> www.rnmrestaurant.com Open dinner Tue–Sat

This sleek, smart room in the Lower Haight combines savoir-faire with a homey simplicity that makes you wish it was your neighborhood hangout. The playful Cal-French menu ranges from mini burgers to sublime concoctions such as seared scallops on cauliflower puree. The early-bird special is a bargain. **Moderate**

Zuni Café *classic Cal-Med cuisine* `3 B4`

1658 Market Street • 415 552 2522

Open lunch & dinner Tue–Sun, brunch Sun

Judy Rodgers' wood-fired Cal-Med cooking has made Zuni an institution, and its warm room has expansive views out onto Market Street. The roast chicken with bread salad is legendary (and requires a wait), as is the burger (lunch only). Brunch is popular, especially if you can score a sidewalk table. **Moderate**

Mecca *industrial chic sophistication*   `3 A5`

2029 Market Street • 415 621 7000
>> www.sfmecca.com Open dinner Tue–Sun

Mecca was one of the first places to inject some spark into the Castro dining scene nearly a decade ago, and it's as stylishly successful as ever. The room is a sophisticated take on warehouse industrial chic, and attracts a well-turned-out crowd. The upscale New American cuisine is reliably delicious. **Moderate**

Chow *high-quality comfort food*   `5 A1`

215 Church Street • 415 552 2469
Open all day from 11am Mon–Fri, from 10am Sat & Sun

For cheap and cheerful comfort food, chow down at this popular Castro hangout. Its simple setting belies the expertise in the kitchen. Roast chicken is crispy and fragrant, steak is perfectly grilled. Adventurous fare like Moroccan-spiced duck succeeds, and the ginger cake with pumpkin ice cream is delicious. **Cheap**

Lime *Castro neighborhood funhouse*   `10 H3`

2247 Market Street • 415 621 5256
>> www.lime-sf.com Open dinner nightly, brunch Sun

This buzzing diner channels the swinging 60s and drags them screaming into the 21st century. Look in through the pink-tinted plate glass windows and you'll see groovy Castro scenesters swarming the cocktail lounge with its gleaming white acrylic ceiling, comfy ottomans, low tables, and sexy servers. A long white marble bar is the centerpiece, inset with personal video monitors and backed by pink mirrors and a "floating" bottle display.

The emphasis here is on cocktail culture, with several kinds of mojitos, numerous other cool libations, and the city's largest selection of vodkas. The fun, small-plate-style food is the perfect accompaniment – deviled eggs, mini burgers, fish tacos, tuna poke, beef short ribs, and the must-have tiny grilled cheese sandwiches with tomato-soup dipping sauce. It's everything needed for a night of fabulous mixing and mingling. **Cheap**

>> *Chestnut Street in the Marina (see p130) is a good bet to browse around if you don't have a reservation*

Restaurants

Town Hall *casual chic fare* `4 G1`
342 Howard Street • 415 908 3900
>> www.townhallsf.com
Open lunch & dinner Mon–Fri, dinner only Sat & Sun

Filling an old warehouse, Town Hall serves New American cuisine with a New Orleans twist. Signature dishes include the flavorful peanut- and tasso-crusted pork chop with smashed potatoes, and roasted duck with dates in gingersnap gravy. **Moderate**

Acme Chophouse *meat perfection* `4 H3`
24 Willie Mays Plaza • 415 644 0240
>> www.acmechophouse.com
Open dinner Tue–Sun, lunch on game days

This steakhouse at the AT&T Park *(see p97)* is a carnivore's heaven. Not only do they make the most succulent steaks you've ever tasted, but they use only naturally raised meats and poultry, local fish, and sustainably grown produce. **Moderate**

Oola Restaurant & Bar *cool bistro* `4 F2`
860 Folsom Street • 415 995 2061
>> www.oola-sf.com
Open dinner nightly (to midnight Sun & Mon, to 1am Tue–Sat)

There's a lively vibe at this smart venue, with its plush booths, modish mezzanine, and accomplished local-producer "American Bistro" fare. Start with a watermelon cosmopolitan and end with the flourless chocolate and raspberry cake. **Moderate**

Dim Sum

Originally the food of Chinese emperors, the tasty steamed dumplings and fried delights known as "dim sum" are ubiquitous and hugely popular in San Francisco, and make an especially enticing weekend brunch option (though many places serve it all day, every day). **Yank Sing** (Map 4 F1, 49 Stevenson St., 415 541 4949, www.yanksing.com) offers some 80 varieties. **Ton Kiang** (Map 7 A5, 5821 Geary Blvd., 415 752 4440, www.tonkiang.net) features Hakka Chinese cuisine with the Hong Kong-style dim sum. **Dol Ho** (Map 1 D4, 808 Pacific Ave., 415 392 2828) serves tasty dim sum at low prices to a mostly local clientele, and **Gold Mountain** (Map 2 E3, 644 Broadway, 415 296 7733) is a bustling, cheap-and-cheerful Chinatown venue.

AsiaSF *gender-bending fusion*

201 9th Street • 415 255 2742
>> www.asiasf.com Open dinner nightly

When your waitress climbs onto the catwalk that bisects this bustling dining room, don't be surprised by the bumping and grinding. After all, this is San Francisco. These beautiful women are actually "gender illusionists" (don't call them drag queens), and several times during a meal, they deliver knockout diva routines to the rowdy crowds. It's hilarious fun, popular with a huge range of customers – bachelor and bachelorette parties, gay groups, couples on a first date, or even a grandmother being feted by her family. A mouthwatering Cal-Asian menu holds its own amid the hoopla. It includes items like sake-steamed mussels, tamarind chicken satay, miso-glazed salmon, and an addictive ahi tuna burger. Walk-ins are taken, but reservations are highly recommended. If you have to wait, saucy cocktails and sake drinks get you in the mood, and there's a dance club downstairs. **Moderate**

La Rondalla *late-night Tijuana*

901 Valencia Street • 415 647 7474
Open dinner nightly, to 2am Fri & Sat

It's always Christmas at this classic Mexican dive in the Mission, which is decked out in tinsel and lights all year round. Locally known for its strong margaritas, live Mariachi players, and late hours, it's lowbrow but gratifying, and authentic dishes like *pozole* and *menudo* satisfy adventurous diners. Cash only. **Cheap**

Ame *Japanese-Italian gem*

689 Mission Street • 415 284 4040
>> www.amerestaurant.com Open lunch & dinner daily

Hiro Sone and Lissa Doumani were not content to rest on the laurels of their acclaimed Napa Valley restaurant, Terra, so they set up Ame in the swank St. Regis hotel. Pristine sashimis and dishes like *spaghettini* with grilled cuttlefish and wild-nettle pesto typify the unique culinary sensibility. **Expensive**

Restaurants

Ti Couz *crepes and café culture* `5 B2`
3108 16th Street • 415 252 7373
Open dinner nightly, lunch Fri–Mon; no reservations

With its charming rustic atmosphere and dozens of varieties of delicious crepes, this little café is always hopping. Savory buckwheat-crepe fillings range from simple parsley butter to smoked salmon. The sweet crepes, made with white flour, might have chocolate or fresh fruits. French hard cider is on tap. **Cheap**

Luna Park *happy hipster hangout* `5 B2`
694 Valencia Street • 415 553 8584
» www.lunaparksf.com
Open dinner nightly, lunch Mon–Fri, brunch Sat & Sun

This trendy eatery on the Valencia corridor is always full of hipsters clamoring for the famous mojitos and fusion food. The retro-style room is decorated with amusement park memorabilia. Signature dishes include goat cheese fondue and do-it-yourself s'mores. **Cheap**

Slow Club *hip comfort food* `6 E2`
2501 Mariposa Street • 415 241 9390
» www.slowclub.com
Open dinner Mon–Sat, lunch Mon–Fri, brunch Sat & Sun

When it opened at the height of the dot-com boom, the Slow Club seemed to typify the time – a hip industrial space with a hypercool clientele and a palpable attitude. Now it has mellowed into one of those rare, consistently comfortable spots you always know you're going to enjoy. It's still hip, but the attitude is gone, and it's taken on a neighborhood feel.

The dark room has a certain glamour, especially in candlelight, with its black walls, concrete floors, and frosted glass windows. The simple Cal-Med menu changes often, but sticks to about half a dozen appetizers and entrees, all expertly prepared. Antipasti change daily – trays of tasty roasted vegetables stand ready on the open kitchen's counters. Reservations are not taken, but the bar is a lively place to wait, with a great cocktail and wine selection. **Cheap**

Levende Lounge *global cuisine* `5 C1`

1710 Mission Street • 415 864 5585
>> www.levendesf.com
Open dinner Tue–Sat, brunch Sun

Trendy types crowd this sexy restaurant and lounge. The room is dressed with overstuffed leather furniture, mahogany tables, amber lighting, and a changing gallery of local art, so it feels intimate despite its size. Delicious cocktails like the Fresa (house-made berry-infused vodka and fresh strawberries) or the Melon (rum with fresh honeydew) let you know that drinks are taken seriously here. The food is also outstanding, mixing Nuevo Latino, Asian, and French influences in small- and large-plate options. And the fun doesn't stop with the food. International DJs spin groovy global music over a state-of-the-art sound system throughout the evening. As it nears midnight, food service stops and the scene takes on a clubbier vibe. On Sundays, there's a party-style "boogie brunch" with a make-it-yourself Bloody Mary bar. **Cheap**

Chez Papa Bistrot *modern Provençal* `6 G2`

1401 18th Street • 415 255 0387
>> www.chezpapasf.com Open dinner nightly, lunch Mon–Sat

This delightful and popular casual bistro brings Provence to Potrero Hill with a "small plates" spin. It bustles day and night, tempting diners with dishes like potato gnocchi with pistou, seared foie gras with quince, and lamb daube. On sunny days, snag one of the few outdoor spots. **Moderate**

Baraka *warm Moroccan boite* `6 F2`

288 Connecticut Street • 415 255 0387
>> www.barakasf.net Open dinner nightly

Baraka serves its acclaimed Moroccan-Mediterranean cuisine in an inviting burnt-orange room with copper and jewel-tone accents. Small- and large-plate options mean you can either graze or settle in with stuffed dates and lamb tartare, or slow-braised short ribs. Several delicious tagines are offered daily. **Moderate**

Restaurants

Foreign Cinema *glam cinematic scene* `5 C3`
2534 Mission Street • 415 648 7600
>> www.foreigncinema.com
Open dinner nightly, brunch Sat & Sun

This hip Cal-Med spot is a glamorous Euro-fantasy tucked away in the Mission district's gritty streets. Amid candlelit tables and patio heaters, in the open courtyard of this converted old theater, foreign films are screened on a brick wall, and snippets of soundtrack drift from drive-in-movie speakers through the night air. Inside, a huge fireplace warms the soaring industrial-chic dining room.

Most folks focus on the food. The cosmopolitan crowd feasts on appetizers like house-cured sardines or beef carpaccio. Entrees might include Moroccan duck breast with quail and chicken sausage or the specialty curry roast chicken. There's a great oyster bar with at least a dozen daily varieties, and a tempting selection of cheeses and decadent desserts. Brunch is outstanding. **Cheap**

Hamano Sushi *for fans of fresh fish* `10 H5`
1332 Castro Street • 415 826 0825
>> www.hamanosushi.com
Open dinner nightly, lunch Tue–Sun

The decor in this no-nonsense Noe Valley Japanese spot is slightly 80s-suburban, but the generous cuts of sushi and sashimi are unbeatable. Maki include creations like the soft-shell crab "spider roll." Arrive early or resign yourself to waiting. **Moderate**

Delfina *rustic Italian* `5 B2`
3621 18th Street • 415 552 4055
Open dinner nightly

Chef Craig Stoll dishes out great-tasting Italian food at this cozy trattoria in the Mission District. Try the *insalata del campo* – bitter greens with pancetta, walnuts, parmesan, and balsamic vinaigrette, or Stoll's signature grilled calamari with warm white beans. Reservations are a must. **Cheap**

Cliff House *historic oceanfront restaurant* `11 A3`

1090 Point Lobos • 415 386 3330

>> www.cliffhouse.com Sutro's and the Bistro open lunch and dinner daily; breakfast daily in the Bistro (brunch Sun); champagne buffet in the Terrace Room 10am–2pm Sun

Few establishments in San Francisco have a more storied history than the famous Cliff House. Sited at Point Lobos, the city's westernmost tip, it's San Francisco's only oceanfront restaurant and overlooks the Seal Rocks (pictured above right) and the Golden Gate.

The original 1863 building was a modest structure that was a favorite recreational destination of the upper classes. After it was destroyed by a fire in 1894, former mayor Adolph Sutro built a Victorian chateau on the site, complete with restaurants and art galleries. Just over a decade later it too was overtaken by fire. In 1909, Sutro's daughter Emma had a simple Neoclassical structure built to house a restaurant. Over the years, the building underwent several remodels and additions, each more graceless than the one before. The place became a mess, but tourists continued to come in droves for the views.

After a $19-million remodel in 2004, the Cliff House finally suits its spectacular site. The original building was carefully restored and retrofitted, and the architects added an audacious modernist wing that houses a new restaurant, called **Sutro's** – a place locals will want to visit along with the tourists.

Sutro's is the unabashed star of the show. The soaring, open room is breathtaking, with 24-ft (7.5-m) tall windows that make the most of the ocean views, and a curving mezzanine that looks down on the bar and dining room as well as out to sea. The menu focuses on American cuisine, and emphasizes seafood, of course, though there is also a range of choice options for carnivores.

The old restaurant, now called **Cliff House Bistro**, is more casual, but also boasts great views. Lighter fare is on offer, and breakfast is served daily, with brunch on Sundays and a champagne buffet in the Terrace Room. The entire complex is decorated with memorabilia from the building's former incarnations and from the adjacent Sutro Baths, which were destroyed in 1963. **Moderate** (Bistro)–**Expensive** (Sutro's)

Chez Panisse *temple to California cuisine*

1517 Shattuck Ave., Berkeley • 510 548 5525 • BART Richmond line to Downtown Berkeley; walk north along Shattuck Ave.
>> www.chezpanisse.com Restaurant open dinner Mon–Sat; café open lunch & dinner Mon–Sat

After more than 30 years, Chez Panisse is still a foodie mecca. Chef Alice Waters runs it as a high temple to just-picked ingredients, environmental harmony, slow cooking, and painstaking presentation. A daily-changing set menu of California cuisine is offered in the warm and woody downstairs restaurant, while an à la carte menu is available in the more casual upstairs café.

This is where the trend for using organic ingredients, local purveyors, and sustainable harvesting first began, and whether you find that admirable or annoying, this is often referred to as America's best restaurant. Menus are based on the availability of the highest-quality products, so the ingredients are the real stars, showcased here as perhaps nowhere else on the planet. **Moderate** (café)–**Expensive** (restaurant)

Zachary's Chicago Pizza *the real deal*

5801 College Ave., Oakland • 510 655 6385
>> www.zacharys.com • BART Pittsburg/Bay Point line to Rockridge Station, then walk half a block north
Open lunch & dinner daily; no reservations

Places worldwide claim to sell "Chicago pizza," but Zachary's gets it right. Stuffed pizzas are saucy, gooey heaven; thin crusts are crisp and toothsome. Specials are offered daily. No reservations, cash only. **Cheap**

Best Bets for Breakfast

If you're hankering for a down-home breakfast, three classic diners are sure to please. **Dottie's True Blue Café** (Map 3 D2, 522 Jones St.) serves portions so huge you can share. **Mama's on Washington Square** (Map 1 D3, 1701 Stockton St.) offers a gourmet take on the classics (brioche French Toast, apple Pan Dore), and **Sears Fine Food** (Map 4 E1, 439 Powell St. www.searsfinefood.com) is famous for fluffy pancakes. Those who prefer a Continental breakfast should try **Tartine Bakery** (Map 5 B2, 600 Guerrero St., www.tartinebakery. com) for simply divine croissants and brioches. At the other end of the spectrum is the decadent Sunday Jazz Brunch at the **Ritz-Carlton Terrace** *(see p152)* set in the hotel's chic courtyard.

East Bay's Gourmet Ghetto

North Berkeley's "Gourmet Ghetto" is the area around Shattuck Avenue between Rose and Hearst Streets. It started in the late 1960s, with the then-revolutionary shops **Peet's Coffee & Tea** (2124 Vine St., www.peets.com) and the **Cheese Board Collective** (1504 Shattuck Ave., www.cheese boardcollective.coop), and is best known as the home of **Chez Panisse** *(see opposite)*, which opened in 1971. You'll also find the terrific **César** tapas bar (1515 Shattuck Ave., 510 883 0222, www.barcesar. com) and the **French Hotel Café** (1538 Shattuck Ave., 510 843 8958). **Juice Bar Collective** (2114 Vine St., 510 548 8473) offers fresh-on-demand juices and quick lunches, while **Masse's Pastries** (1469 Shattuck Ave., 510 649 1004) is French pastry perfection.

A Côte *trendy French tapas*
5478 College Ave., Oakland • 510 655 6469 • BART Pittsburg/ Bay Point line to Rockridge Station, then walk one block south
≫ www.acoterestaurant.com Open dinner nightly

Oakland's hot Rockridge neighborhood *(see p135)* is home to this charming, wildly popular French small-plates place. Service is tapas-bar style, so dishes are delivered as they're ready and are meant to be shared. No reservations are taken. **Moderate**

Sam's Anchor Café *seafood and views* ✓
27 Main St., Tiburon • 415 435 4527 • Blue & Gold Fleet ferry from Pier 41 Open lunch & dinner daily, brunch Sat & Sun
≫ www.samscafe.com

Classic American seafood, steaks, burgers, sandwiches, and microbrew beers are served on a huge deck looking back toward the city, making this a very popular weekend hangout. Have one of their famous Ramos Fizzes and soak up the sun. **Cheap**

Sushi Ran *luxe sushi and sake*
107 Caledonia Street, Sausalito • 415 332 3620 • Golden Gate Transit bus No. 10 to Bridgeway and Turney Sts. in Sausalito
≫ www.sushiran.com Open dinner nightly, lunch Mon–Fri

Monied Marin County crowds come here for the exquisite, pristine Cal-Japanese food. The place makes for good people-watching, and serves truly stunning sushi. A quintessential North Bay experience. Reserve early or crowd into the wine bar. **Expensive**

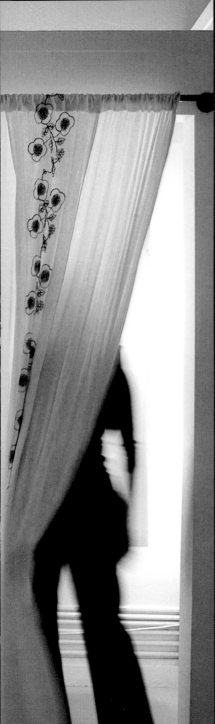

shopping

San Francisco is an exciting shopping destination, with its fabulous selection of stores, from the *haute couture* boutiques around Union Square to the edgy and avant-garde Hayes Valley. Sacramento Street is where society mavens browse for elegant home furnishings, while upper Grant Avenue is the latest favorite of local fashionistas. Whether you're after the best bakery or a bohemian bookstore, you'll find it here.

SHOPPING

San Francisco's shopping scene is one of the best in the country, with lots of great neighborhood stores as well as well-known hubs. Union Square is known for its *haute couture* (don't miss Maiden Lane), while Hayes Valley offers cutting-edge fashion in a funky locale and the Mission has lots of local color and indie designs. Trendy Fillmore Street and the Marina are ideal for warm-weather browsing, and offer plenty of sidewalk cafés for pit stops.

Kristine Carber

Foodie Finds

San Francisco has plenty of fine food stores catering to locals' upmarket tastes. Many feel that **XOX Truffles** *(see p54)* makes the best chocolate on the West Coast, and **Cowgirl Creamery** *(see p52)* has the best artisan cheese. Over at **Hog Island Oyster Co.** *(see p52)*, you can buy mollusks that are served at the city's top restaurants and wine bars.

Interior Solutions

Downtown **Gump's** *(see p54)* is the city's best-known store for exquisite *objets* for the home, though **Sue Fisher King** *(see p59)* is also famous for stylish accessories and gifts. More unusual housewares are sold at **The Gardener** *(see p65)* in Berkeley, while **Bauerware Cabinet Hardware** *(see p62)* stocks a whimsical and traditional selection of goods.

It's a Man's World

West Coast men's fashion is not just about surfer style and vintage threads. Both **Wilkes Bashford** *(see p55)* and **David Stephen** *(see p55)* offer Italian apparel, and at **Nida** *(see p58)* gents can find cutting-edge labels from Jet and Helmut Lang. San Francisco is also where **The Gap** *(see p61)* and its legendary casual look started out.

choice shops

Retro Retail

The city has a great range of outlets for vintage homewares and apparel. Even high-fashion Pacific Heights offers retro options. For furnishings with a French country feel try **Nest** *(see p56)* or **Brown Dirt Cowboy's** *(see p54)*. On Haight Street, bargain hunters enjoy the numerous vintage stores such as **La Rosa** (No. 1711) or **Wasteland** (No. 1660).

Designer Clothes

Fashionistas will find much to satiate their sartorial needs on Sacramento Street. **Susan** *(see p61)* is a must for cutting-edge runway style, while **Grocery Store** *(see p61)* stocks cheaper second labels and **Goodbyes** *(see p60)* is an *haute-couture* consignment store. **Azalea** *(see p58)* offers edgy fashions from young U.S. and local designers.

Shoes and Accessories

To tackle the city's hills, sneakers are the way to go, but you can step out in Italian style if you go to **Paolo** *(see p58)* or **Bulo** *(see p58)*. Also on Hayes Street, **Gimme Shoes** *(see p58)* stocks more daring European shoes, plus belts and purses. To top things off, try **Mrs. Dewson's Hats** *(see p57)*, a landmark for handmade headgear.

Ferry Building Marketplace

The Embarcadero and Market Street • 415 693 0996
>> www.ferrybuildingmarketplace.com
Open 10–6 Mon–Fri, 9–6 Sat, 11–5 Sun

Built in 1896, the Ferry Building was once the gateway to the city, receiving millions of ferry passengers every year. Today, shoppers flock here to buy and consume high-quality foodstuffs. A good place to start is **Peet's Coffee & Tea** (No. 43, www.peets.com), the premier gourmet roastery known for its intense European-style coffee. **Scharffen Berger Chocolate Maker** (No. 14, www.scharffenberger.com) makes some of the finest chocolate in the country, while **Recchiuti Confections** (No. 30, www.recchiuticonfections.com) stocks artisan Michael Recchiuti's handmade candy.

Hog Island Oyster Co. (No. 11, www.hogisland oysters.com) is a bar and retail outlet where you'll find quite possibly the finest oysters on the West Coast,

with varieties like Belons, Kumamotos, and Hog's own Sweetwaters. **Tsar Nicoulai Caviar** (No. 12, www.tsarnicoulai.com) is a combination café and boutique where you can sample the delicious fish eggs before buying. Products include domestic and imported caviar as well as smoked sturgeon and salmon.

Cowgirl Creamery's Artisan Cheese Shop (No. 17, www.cowgirlcreamery.com) has a cult following for its handmade organic cheeses. Try the world-famous triple-cream Red Hawk, which goes well with the French or sourdough baguettes from **Acme Bread Company** (No. 15, 415 288 2978), voted number one bread-maker in the Bay Area in a local magazine survey.

McEvoy Ranch Olive Oil (No. 16, www.mcevoy ranch.com) is known for its peppery oils produced in Marin County. For organic fruit, don't miss **Frog Hollow Farm** (No. 46, www.froghollow.com), which also sells homemade chutneys, marmalades, and pastries.

Jackson Square *antiques enclave* `2 E4`
Jackson Street and Hotaling Place
>> www.jacksonsquaresf.com

Once San Francisco's bawdy Barbary Coast, Jackson Square is today a delightful enclave of Federalist-style storefronts housing antique furniture and decorative arts. **Thomas Livingston Antiques** (550 Jackson St., www.thomaslivingstonantiques.com) specializes in Georgian and Regency pieces. Those looking for silver trinkets should head to **Argentum – The Leopard's Head** (472 Jackson St., www.argentum-theleopard.com), devoted to pieces dating from the 17th century. For Spanish and Italian Baroque tables and chests, make your way to **Foster-Gwin Inc.** (38 Hotaling Place, www.fostergwin.com), housed in an old livery stable. **Daniel Stein Antiques** (458 Jackson St., www.danielsteinantiques.com) stocks 18th- and 19th-century English furnishings and art, while European furniture is the specialty at **Dillingham & Company** (432 Jackson St., www.dillinghamandcompany.com).

City Lights *iconic independent bookstore* `2 E4`
261 Columbus Avenue • 415 362 8193
>> www.citylights.com Open 10am–midnight daily

If Allen Ginsberg were alive, he would still be hanging out at this North Beach icon opened in 1953 by poet Lawrence Ferlinghetti. Once a mecca for Beat poets and writers who penned their works in nearby cafés, the store now attracts book-lovers who leaf through titles on art, philosophy, and bohemian poetry and fiction.

AB Fits *designer jeans for every shape* `2 E3`
1519 Grant Avenue • 415 982 5726
>> www.abfits.com Open 11–6:30 Tue–Sat, noon–6 Sun

This fashion-forward boutique on trendy upper Grant Avenue offers an incredible selection of hip cotton and knit tops as well as designer jeans. Owners Howard Gee and Christopher Louie take pride in finding the right style for the individual customer, from labels such as Earnest Sewn, Chip & Pepper, Kasil, and Nudie.

>> *Most vendors at the Ferry Building Marketplace ship, so you can enjoy your favorite finds at home* `53`

XOX Truffles *decadent chocolate treats* `1 D3`
754 Columbus Avenue • 415 421 4814
▶▶ www.xoxtruffles.com Open 9–6 Mon–Sat

Decked out in the blues and yellows of Provence, this confectioner carries quite possibly the best chocolate in the city. It is owned by a French chef and his wife, who started out supplying their truffles to hotels and caterers. They were so popular that the couple opened this shop offering 27 varieties, like cognac and caramel.

Brown Dirt Cowboy's *irresistible gifts* `1 B3`
2406 Polk Street • 415 922 9065
Open 12:30–6:30 Wed–Mon

Named for an Elton John song, Brown Dirt Cowboy's is housed in a Victorian building with an ivy-decked entry. The shop started by selling refurbished armoires and chests, and has expanded to include reupholstered furniture from the 1920s and 30s. Colorful pots, tiles, and dainty towels are other treasures to covet.

Gump's *icon of elegance* `4 E1`
135 Post Street • 415 982 1616
▶▶ www.gumps.com Open 10–6 Mon–Sat, noon–5 Sun

Gump's is housed in a magnificent pillared landmark dating to 1910, with an 18th-century Ch'ing dynasty buddha at the entrance. Originally founded as a mirror and framing shop, Gump's has evolved into the city's premier destination for antiques and *objets d'art.*

Today the store has the world's best selection of china, crystal, and tableware. It is renowned for its jade, coral, and pearl jewelry as well as its collection of Baccarat and Steuben crystal. The bridal registry is one of the finest in the country, offering table linens, silver flatware, and some 400 patterns of china. Oriental influences include the koi and bamboo vases, and the Chinese blossom motif on textiles and screens.

Wilkes Bashford *boldly conservative* 4 E1

375 Sutter Street • 415 986 4380
>> www.wilkesbashford.com Open 10–6 Mon–Sat (to 8 Thu)

Fine clothier Wilkes Bashford has dressed three
generations of San Franciscans in sleek Italian suits,
sportswear, and leather shoes. Spread over six levels
are the sophisticated designs of Brioni, Oxxford
Clothes, and Kiton, as well as women's couture
bearing the labels of Oscar de la Renta and Valentino.

Britex Fabrics *gorgeous textiles* 4 E1

146 Geary Street • 415 392 2910

>> www.britexfabrics.com
Open 9:30–6 Mon–Sat, noon–5 Sun

Opened in 1952, this family-run fabric emporium has
four floors of trims, fabric, and sewing paraphernalia.
Look for woolens, French lace, and elegant silks and
chiffons. The 3rd floor has 30,000 antique and new
buttons, and the 4th floor features discounted offcuts.

Maiden Lane *designer haven* 4 E1

Maiden Lane is a Parisian-like alleyway near Union
Square lined with chic boutiques. At **De Vera** (No. 29,
www.deveraobjects.com) you'll find Federico de Vera's
elegant glassware as well as his jewelry creations.
David Stephen (No. 50, www.davidstephen.com) is
one of the oldest men's stores in the city, and
specializes in hand-tailored suits and sportswear

from Italian designers. **Tse** (No. 60, www.tsecashmere.
com) purveys exquisite cashmere.

Cross the alley and you'll come to **Marc Jacobs**
(No. 125, www.marcjacobs.com), with casual but high-
fashion attire, as well as **Yves Saint Laurent** (No. 166,
www.ysl.com), with its hallmark silks, cottons, and
leather. **Diptyque** (No. 171, www.diptyqueusa.com) is
the place for gorgeous candles handmade in Paris.

>> *Wilkes Bashford has a full bar on each floor, serving complimentary cocktails, coffee, or sodas to shoppers* **55**

Shopping

Sumbody *natural pampering* 8 H3
2167 Union Street • 415 775 6343
>> www.sumbody.com
Open 10:30–6:30 Mon–Thu, 10–7 Fri & Sat, 11–6 Sun

With names like Dream Time Bath Salts and Foot Fizzer, the handmade, all-natural bath, body, and home spa products at this northern California-based company are very enticing. The range extends from moisturizers to scrubs, facial masks, and baby products.

Nest *French country homewares* 8 H4
2300 Fillmore Street • 415 292 6199
Open 10:30–6:30 Mon–Sat, 11–6 Sun

A charming boutique, where shoppers browse real and reproduction antiques sourced at flea markets in Paris and Provence. The shop is filled with handmade linens, ceramics, dainty slippers, and decorative items. David Bowie and Anne Heche are among the celebrities who have browsed the well-stocked shelves.

Toujours *soft and irresistible lingerie* 8 H4
2484 Sacramento Street • 415 346 3988
>> www.toujourslingerie.com Open 11–6 Mon–Sat, noon–5 Sun

Owner Beverly Weinkauf keeps this tidy shop packed with romantic lingerie from high-end names like Cotton Club. Hanro Falke's deluxe hosiery is stocked, as are bustiers, corsets, and lacy garters. There is a mail-order service for reordering, and in October major reductions are offered on seasonal lines.

Department Stores
Of all the great shopping destinations in San Francisco, none matches the sophistication of Union Square (Map 4 E1). The first department store opened here in 1896, and since then the square has become a mecca for fine shopping.

Today you'll find **Macy's** (251 Geary Street, www.macys.com), the third-largest department store in the world, as well as **Neiman Marcus** (150 Stockton Street, www.neimanmarcus.com) and **Saks Fifth Avenue** (384 Post Street, www.saksfifth avenue.com), both known for exquisite haute couture.

Nearby is **Nordstrom** (865 Market Street, www. nordstrom.com), offering apparel, more than 1,000 pairs of shoes, and its own private spa. The spiral escalator is one of only a handful in the world.

Hydra *fresh and fragrant*   `8 H4`
1919 Fillmore Street • 415 474 9372
>> www.hydrasoap.com
Open 10:30–8 Sun–Thu (to 9 Fri & Sat)

This mega-popular store is filled with bins of natural soaps sporting names like strawberry daiquiri, piña colada, and martini. All manner of sponges, lotions, and scrubs are also for sale. Look out for the barrel of rubber ducks near the outsize bath tub.

Zinc Details *retro-style furnishings*   `8 H4`
1905 Fillmore Street • 415 776 2100
>> www.zincdetails.com Open 11–7 Mon–Sat, noon–6 Sun

A longtime favorite for contemporary interpretations of minimalist 1950s and 60s designs, as well as Japanese and Scandinavian classics. Expect to find sleek birch chests, rice-paper lamps, modern Danish consoles, distinctive Ikebana vases, and stylish homewares, including Miam-Miam mugs.

Mrs. Dewson's Hats *elegant toppers*   `8 H4`
2050 Fillmore Street • 415 346 1600
>> www.mrsdewsonhats.com Open 11–6 Tue–Sun

Hats trimmed in elegant silk, lace, or rosettes are the specialty at this tiny gem on fashionable Fillmore Street, opened in 1978 by the flamboyant Ruth Garland-Dewson. Most hats are handmade and hand-dyed (including some designed by Dewson herself), and bedecked with big floppy flowers or real fur and feathers. The black felt with red ostrich feathers is the most popular winter hat for women, but in spring and summer the shop is pleasingly crammed with a dazzling selection of chapeaux in all colors and styles, including broad rims, berets, and chantrelles in yellows, pinks, blues, and greens. Men can choose from old-fashioned boaters, bowlers, Biltmores, and Panamas, plus the famous "Willie" fedora, available in three sizes and named for San Francisco's former mayor, a long-time fan of the shop. Movie stars Sharon Stone and Billy Dee Williams often drop by when visiting the city.

>> *Maiden Lane (see p55) is one of the few places in the city with summertime sidewalk cafés*

Shopping

Hayes Street *hip shopping neighborhood* 3 B4

Hayes Street is one of the city's favorite success stories. For years a rundown strip of bars and liquor stores, the area has been transformed into a trendy enclave of ultra-hip boutiques, cafés, and restaurants.

Start at **Bulo** (Nos. 418 and 437a, www.buloshoes.com). The name is Perugian for "hip," which describes the selection of Italian shoes from designers like OXS and Krizia. **Gimme Shoes** (No. 416, www.gimmeshoes.com) also caters to the trendsetting crowd with its avant-garde European footwear, unusual athletic shoes, and designer accessories.

One-of-a-kind shoes, belts, purses, and gloves are to be found at **Paolo** (No. 524, www.paoloshoes.com), where the styles range from classic to edgy. Don't miss the Venetian murals and masks reflecting owner Paolo Iantorno's travels in Italy.

At **Alabaster** (No. 597, www.alabastersf.com) Old World accents and imports are the draw, including alabaster, ceramics, and Art Deco furniture from 1920s France. **Friend** (No. 401, www.friend-sf.com) is an inviting design store that showcases new and established talent, while **Flight 001** (No. 525, www.flight001.com) is shaped like the hull of a cabin and bedecked with racks displaying bags and pillows.

The baby-blue façade and tangerine walls of **Nida** (No. 564) make a bright backdrop for the trendy apparel from Marc by Marc Jacobs and Vanessa Bruno. Also carrying emerging and established labels is **Azalea** (No. 411, www.azaleasf.com), which stocks a range of styles, and has its own nail bar. Japanese rice wine is the specialty at **True Sake** (No. 560, www.truesake.com), America's first store dedicated to the drink. Prices range from $18 to $200 per bottle.

Sue Fisher King *elegant and refined*   `8 G4`

3067 Sacramento Street • 415 922 7276
>> www.suefisherking.com Open 10–6 Mon–Sat

Nestled in the peaceful, tree-shaded Pacific Heights neighborhood, Sue Fisher King carries exquisite homewares and gifts that have pleased even the most finicky shoppers since 1978. The store was opened to pay for King's travels to Europe, and it was so popular that she soon expanded to include Italian goods, paying homage to her love of the country.

Besides pillows and trinkets, there are luxury Italian sheets in creamy damasks and cotton as well as hand-blocked velvet from Venice and silk coverlets by Mirella Spinella. Anichini's gorgeous bedding in tapestry and brocade is also on sale. One area is dedicated to fluffy towels, mats, and robes. Elegant glazed white dinnerware and hand-painted Sienna pottery inspired by medieval designs are always in stock, as well as Fortuny lamps with silk tassels and hand-painted silk shades. Regular buying trips to Europe keep merchandise fashionable and fresh, and during the holidays King fills shelves with decorations from more than 30 different countries.

Museum Stores

Some of San Francisco's finest art and gift shops can be found in its museums. The MuseumStore at the **San Francisco Museum of Modern Art** *(see p78)* attracts those seeking contemporary works of art, like Alvar Aalto's hallmark vases and contemporary dinnerware inspired by the museum's design. It also stocks books, posters, and jewelry.

For ethnic crafts, head to the **Museum of Craft and Folk Art** *(see p74)* where you can choose from contemporary functional and decorative objects. **The Museo ItaloAmericano**, located in the Fort Mason Center *(see p73)*, is a treasure trove of Italian ceramics, jewelry, and Venetian glass.

The store at the **Asian Art Museum** *(see p70)* is a repository of high-quality Asian porcelain, textiles, antiques, and new furniture. Their unique merchandise complements current exhibits.

At the **Legion of Honor** *(see pp80–81)* there are works relating to both the permanent collection and special exhibits, with Art Deco-style glassware and tabletop sculptures.

The **California Historical Society** (Map 4 F1, 678 Mission St., www.californiahistoricalsociety.org) has the city's best selection of books on local history, with topics from Coit Tower to the Barbary Coast.

Those looking for quirkier gifts might find them at **The Exploratorium** (Map 8 F2, 3601 Lyon Street, www.exploratorium.edu), where science-related games and art are the mainstay; or at the **Cartoon Art Museum** *(see p74)*, which stocks hard-to-find comic books and posters.

>> *Union Square art galleries open late the first Thursday of the month and serve wine for aspiring collectors*   `59`

Shopping

Sarah Shaw *classic clothes with an edge* 8 G4
3095 Sacramento Street • 415 929 2990
» www.sarahshaw.com Open 11–6 Mon–Sat, 11–5 Sun

Former Levi Strauss designer Sarah Shaw's shop is a welcome change from the abundance of sterile, minimalist boutiques in the Pacific Heights area. Fresh orchids and a comfy sofa and chairs set the mood for leisurely browsing through racks of clothing from top American designers like Trina Turk, Red Engine, and Julie Brown, whose silk print dresses and halters sell out as soon as they arrive in the shop.

Shaw opened the boutique in 1999 when she couldn't find colorful yet sophisticated career apparel. The look is hip, yet classic enough to wear in a professional setting, and although the emphasis is on separates and jeans, there's a good representation of cocktail dresses and gowns, too. Also stocked are attractive leather purses from Trina Turk and Lamarthe, Hanky Panky underwear, and an enticing selection of jewelry.

Goodbyes *designs at a discount* 8 F4
3464 (men's) & 3483 (women's) Sacramento St.
» www.goodbyessf.com • 415 346 6388 & 674 0151
Open 10–6 Mon–Sat (to 8 Thu), 11–5 Sun

Bargain-hunters love this consignment shop for its incredible finds, including Donna Karan, Armani, Polo/Ralph Lauren, and other haute couture. Racks at its two stores are pleasantly crammed with clothes and accessories, all in excellent condition.

Divine Girls *one-stop fashion* 8 F4
344 Presidio Avenue • 415 409 4901
» www.divinegirls.net Open 10–6 Mon–Sat

From the most basic T-shirt to the most stylish evening dress, this high-end women's boutique caters to fashionistas of all ages. Among the designer labels are Roland Mouret and Alberta Ferretti, with looks ranging from classic to edgy. Complete the outfit with footwear and accessories from a stylish range.

Susan *trendsetting labels* `8 E4`
3685 Sacramento Street • 415 922 3685
Open 10:30–6:30 Mon–Fri, 10:30–6 Sat

Balenciaga, Marni, Jil Sander, and Lanvin are a few of the labels carried at this hip Pacific Heights boutique, where the emphasis is on cutting-edge runway fashion from up-and-coming European and Japanese designers. Shoes and purses from the likes of Jimmy Choo and Prada are also stocked.

Green Apple Books *bibliophile's dream* `7 D5`
506 Clement Street • 415 387 2272
>> www.greenapplebooks.com ✓
Open 10am–10:30pm Sun–Thu, 10am–11:30pm Fri & Sat

Green Apple Books offers the largest selection of used books in the city, with more than 100,000 titles, plus 60,000 new books and magazines. The store, which opened nearly 40 years ago, occupies a turn-of-the-century building with the original creaky floors and maze-like setting and stocks titles covering everything from comics to covered bridges. Sure, there are lots of chain booksellers in the city, but the fun of shopping at Green Apple is in rubbing elbows with surfers, techies, and Pacific Heights doyennes, and poking through the bargain bins and floor-to-ceiling shelves stacked with new arrivals. The friendly, knowledgeable staff love to share good reads, and there are signs throughout the shop with their recommendations. Don't miss the wooden leprechaun at the entry, bestowing good luck on those who rub his tummy as they pass.

Flagship Stores

Several retail giants have flagship stores in the city, housed in historic buildings. **Banana Republic** (Map 4 E1, 256 Grant Ave., www.bananarepublic.com) takes up a city block with its sporty men's and women's slacks, shorts, and T-shirts. At **The Gap** (Map 4 E2, 890 Market St., www.gap.com) you'll find the signature "Gap casual" look and twists on old classics. **Diesel** (Map 4 E1, 101 Post St., www.diesel.com) is packed with trendy apparel, including skirts, jackets, and hundreds of denim pants in various cuts. Head to **Old Navy** (Map 4 E2, 801 Market St., www.oldnavy.com) for three floors of well-priced clothing, or to **Levi's** (Map 4 E1, 300 Post St., www.levistrauss.com) for an awe-inspiring selection of the hallmark jeans and jackets.

Shopping

Amoeba Music *vast music emporium*

10 E2

1855 Haight Street • 415 831 1200
>> www.amoebamusic.com
Open 10:30–10 Mon–Sat and 11–9 Sun

This bustling Haight-Ashbury repository of music is as popular for people-watching as it is for buying, selling, and trading CDs, videos, and tapes. The collection of 500,000 new and used discs is well organized and represents every musical style, from roots to rap.

Say Cheese *foodie heaven*

10 F3

856 Cole Street • 415 665 5020
Open 10–7 Mon–Sat, 10–5 Sun

Known for its French goat's cheeses, this Cole Valley gem carries more than 200 other cheeses, including the hard-to-find Brillat-Savarin (a triple cream cheese named for an 18th-century food writer) and a rare Italian sheep's milk cheese with porcini and black truffles. Caviar, tortes, and 12 kinds of pâté are also stocked.

Bauerware Cabinet Hardware

10 H3

3886 17th Street • 415 864 3886
>> www.bauerware.com Open 9–6 Mon–Sat

Owned by local designer Lou Ann Bauer, this boutique features three walls of trays brimming with traditional and contemporary drawer pulls, decorative knobs, and handles. Styles range from Victorian and Art Deco glass to Baccarat crystal at $1,500 a pair. The mah jong tile and snooker ball are among the quirkier designs.

Metreon *hi-tech entertainment complex*

4 E2

101 4th Street • 415 369 6000
>> www.metreon.com Open 10–10 daily

This glass megaplex houses shops and restaurants and a 15-screen movie theater with the city's only IMAX theater. Among the places to browse are SonyStyle, for cutting-edge audio and visual products, and PlayStation, an interactive game store where hands-on is the motto. Chronicle Books and Gifts to Go are also worth checking out. Don't miss the breathtaking view of Yerba Buena Gardens *(see p143)* from the third level.

Bell'occhio *beautiful gifts* 3 B4
8 Brady Street • 415 864 4048
≫ www.bellocchio.com Open 11–5 Tue–Sat

Tucked down a quiet side street, Bell'occhio is a charming French-style boutique selling antiques and gifts made in European ateliers. Distressed wood-plank floors and high ceilings create a warm setting in which to browse the silk flowers, decorative boxes, and exquisite antique and reproduction ribbons. (Kate Winslet's gloves in the movie *Titanic* were trimmed with the store's black and white ribbon.)

Claudia Schwartz opened the store nearly 20 years ago and keeps it stocked with beautiful and refined pieces, including special lotions and toiletries from European boutiques. LeClerc cosmetics are popular for their luxurious powders and scents. Other favorites are the Santa Maria Novella lotions and soaps. Potpourri, cologne, and candles are also for sale. For pure indulgence, don't miss the handmade chocolates from Incroyables and Rococo Artisan.

Dandelion *cozy and stylish* 6 E1
55 Potrero Avenue • 415 436 9500
≫ www.tampopo.com Open 10–6 Tue–Sat

There's something comforting about browsing this gift and home accessories store. It's as if you've stepped into a living room filled with special treasures from the owner's travels. There are nooks devoted to Paris and Venice and showcasing lovely photos, linens, and tableware. Other sections are devoted to the outdoors and artisan foods.

The owners make regular trips abroad, buying only what they love and then importing directly to keep prices down. The shop is a perennial favorite for one-of-a-kind finds, and a loyal following – many of whom are now friends as well as clients – come here to check out the rare Limoges boxes, stylish totes, and trendy Art Deco-style glasses. Bamboo and woven mats are staples, and slate tabletop fountains are also stocked. The 2nd floor, devoted to design books, is arranged as a library with an inviting overstuffed sofa to rest on.

Shopping

Sunhee Moon *retro-inspired style* `5 B2`
3167 16th Street • 415 355 1800
>> www.sunheemoon.com
Open noon–7 Mon–Fri, noon–6 Sat & Sun

Women looking to add style to their wardrobe should stop by local fashion designer Sunhee Moon's small, hip specialty boutique in the Mission. Influenced by the classic lines of the 1950s, her simple, very clean designs include fitted tees and flared stretchy pants.

Rabat *foot fashion for men and women* `10 H5`
4001 24th Street • 415 282 7861
>> www.rabatshoes.com
Open 10–6:30 Mon–Fri, 10–6 Sat, 11–5:30 Sun

Shoppers who want to stay ahead of the trends make regular pilgrimages to Rabat to check out the edgy but chic designer footwear from New York and Europe. Look for pumps, pointy heels, and even sneakers, as well as purses and jewelry by local artists.

George *everything for furry friends*
1844 4th Street, Berkeley • 510 644 1033 • BART to North Berkeley, then No. 51 AC Transit bus to 3rd and University
>> www.georgesf.com Open 10–6 Mon–Sat, 11–6 Sun

Fashion hounds flock to this mega-popular dog and cat boutique for pet paraphernalia which includes ceramic bowls, whimsical toys, quilts, dog biscuits, and stylish collars and leashes.

The shop is owned by former New Yorker Bobby Wise, who moved to San Francisco and couldn't find decent canine supplies or clothing for his wire-hair fox terrier, George. So he started designing his own, making them as pleasing to look at as to wear. In 1991 George opened its doors, and today four-legged fashionistas and their owners browse through piles of bedding, jackets, and hats in all styles, patterns, and colors. Colorful feeding accessories are also for sale and can be filled with baked-from-scratch biscuits and treats. Visit in January to find discounted doggy raincoats and sweaters.

The Gardener *cultivating style*
1836 4th Street, Berkeley • 510 548 4545 • BART to North
Berkeley, then No. 51 AC Transit bus to 3rd and University
>> www.thegardener.com Open 10–6 Mon–Sat, 11–6 Sun

Located on trendy 4th Street, this shrine to the home
and garden was founded more than 20 years ago by
avid gardener Alta Tingle, who wanted to showcase
gardening tools and accessories not found anywhere
else. The shop has since expanded to feature
imported furnishings and accents, including chunky
wooden tables and chairs, Pakistani urns, French
candles, and fine Belgian linens.

The Italian ceramics are big sellers, and range from
brightly colored tableware and platters to tureens and
vases. Also for sale are hand-carved wooden bowls from
South Africa. Everything is stylishly displayed in the
open, airy space. There's also a front patio dedicated
to outdoor furniture such as Adirondacks, deck chairs,
and redwood chaises. A special garden section offers
books, rare orchids, gloves, and garden-motif gifts.

Margaret O'Leary *handmade woollens*
1832 4th Street, Berkeley • 510 540 8241 • BART to North
Berkeley, then No. 51 AC Transit bus to 3rd and University
>> www.margaretoleary.com Open 10–6 Mon–Sat, 11–6 Sun

This Irish-born designer hand-looms stylish sweaters
and tops in a variety of fabrics, colors, and styles. The
cashmere and seasonal mohair cardigans are especially
worth noting, as is the new line of sportswear. Designs
from Rozae Nicols and Jill Platner are also stocked.

Tail of the Yak *innovative and colorful crafts*
2632 Ashby Ave., Berkeley • 510 841 9891 • BART to
Rockridge Station in Oakland, then No. 51 AC Transit bus to
College and Ashby Open 11–5:30 Mon–Sat

Lavender walls and hardwood floors make a pleasant
backdrop for the lovely gifts at this 30-year-old shop.
The store stocks handmade boxes, glassware, and
antique *santo* figurines from Mexico and Central
America. Vintage European jewelry is a specialty.

art & architecture

San Francisco will always be associated with Victorian houses, but the city has much more to offer than "painted ladies." Some of the country's most beautiful Beaux-Arts buildings are here, as well as fine examples of Arts and Crafts and Art Deco architecture. With some of the finest art museums and an ever-growing gallery scene, the city offers a wealth of culture to explore.

ART AND ARCHITECTURE

The city's art scene has become much more exciting in the past decade, thanks in part to some fantastic redesigns for a couple of its major museums. But I still love to revisit less-heralded destinations like Oakland's Chapel of the Chimes or downtown's splendid Xanadu Gallery. I'm also a big fan of the Legion of Honor – as much for its stunning setting as for what's on show – and late-night openings, when even a familiar museum takes on a whole new aspect.

Peter Cieply

Beaux-Arts Beauties

San Francisco boasts many fine examples of Beaux-Arts architecture. **City Hall** *(see p71)* is one of the nation's best, and incorporates French Renaissance-style features. Opposite, the **SF War Memorial Opera House** *(see p92)* was conceived to harmonize with it. The attractive **Palace of Fine Arts** *(see p73)* is one of the city's most beloved icons.

Major Art Museums

The museum scene here has something for everyone. Fans of modern art adore **SFMOMA** *(see p78)*; aficionados of Eastern art are awed by the **Asian Art Museum** *(see p70)*, one of the largest such collections in the West; the **Legion of Honor** *(see pp80–81)*, is a jewel box of art treasures; and the **de Young Museum** *(see p79)* is red hot in its stunning new home.

Best Exhibition Spaces

In addition to the major museums, you'll find arresting temporary exhibits at the **Yerba Buena Center for the Arts** *(see p74)*, which specializes in cutting-edge art; at **New Langton Arts** *(see p75)*, with its new works by local and international visual artists; and at the many established art galleries at 49 Geary Street *(see p71)*.

choice sights

Art in the Open

For some fresh air with your art, take a walk. The **Precita Eyes Mural Arts and Visitors' Center** *(see p75)* conducts tours of Mission-district murals, while various tours of **Victorian architecture** *(see p72)* focus on the city's signature style. Further afield, the garden of the **Cantor Arts Center** *(see p78)* has the largest collection of Rodin sculptures outside Paris.

Style Icons

The Bay Area offers several true architectural masterpieces. Frank Lloyd Wright's striking **Xanadu Gallery** *(see p70)* anticipated his New York Guggenheim Museum design. The **Paramount Theatre** in Oakland *(see p82)* is an Art Deco palace, and **The Beach Chalet** *(see p82)*, a perfect Arts and Crafts specimen, is filled with unique Depression-era frescoes.

Spiritual Retreats

If you're feeling contemplative, seek out one of these soothing spaces. **Mission Dolores** *(see p75)* was built in 1776 and its graveyard appeared in Hitchcock's *Vertigo*. The Neo-Gothic **Grace Cathedral** *(see p71)* boasts a rose window made in Chartres, and across the bay, the **Chapel of the Chimes** *(see p83)* has a surprisingly beautiful series of cloisters.

Art & Architecture

Xanadu Gallery *Lloyd Wright gem* `4 E1`
140 Maiden Lane • 415 392 9999
>> www.xanadugallery.us Open 10–6 Mon–Sat

San Francisco's only Frank Lloyd Wright-designed building is a miniature masterpiece, with a curving ramp that recalls New York's Guggenheim Museum and a cast-plastic bubble ceiling that evokes Wright's famous Johnson Wax building. The gallery itself is a high-end shop for exotic arts, jewelry, and antiquities.

Tin How Temple *Buddhist place of worship* `2 E4`
125 Waverly Place, 3rd floor
Open 10–5 daily, donation requested

This incense-scented temple on Waverly Place is a world away from the tourist-teeming sidewalks of Chinatown. It is the oldest Chinese temple in the US, founded in 1852. Up three flights of stairs past two mah jong parlors, the narrow room contains beautiful gold-leaf wood carvings and hundreds of red and gold lanterns.

Asian Art Museum *treasure from the East* `3 C3`
200 Larkin Street • 415 581 3500
>> www.asianart.org Open 10–5 Tue–Sun (to 9 Thu)

The Asian Art Museum, one of the largest museums of its kind in the Western world, reopened in 2003 in its stunning new home. San Francisco's former Main Library building was gutted and redesigned by Italian architect Gae Aulenti (famous for the Musée d'Orsay in Paris) to make a handsome setting for the city's greatest art collection. A skylit court with a majestic staircase forms a central public area onto which many galleries open, conveying a grand sense of space.

The galleries are arranged geographically, using the spread of Buddhism throughout Asia as an organizing principle. The collections include some 15,000 objects ranging from tiny jade carvings to monumental sculptures, paintings, porcelains, armor, and puppets. Besides its wealth of ancient objects, the museum is also noted for including contemporary works. **Adm**

City Hall *Beaux-Arts masterpiece* `3 C3`
1 Dr. Carlton B. Goodlett Place • 415 554 4000
» www.sfgov.org/site/cityhall Open 8–8 Mon–Fri

This 1915 Beaux-Arts beauty is acknowledged as one of the country's finest examples of French Renaissance-style architecture. The dome is the largest in North America and the fifth largest in the world.

A retrofit after the 1989 earthquake enhanced the building's beauty and made it an engineering marvel. It now "floats" on shock absorbers and is surrounded by a moat that allows it to move as much as 26 inches (66 cm) without damage in an earthquake. Its decor has been painstakingly restored – some 30,000 pieces of marble were removed, cleaned, and replaced, and the dome was trimmed with gold leaf.

City Hall has famously been the site of numerous weddings, including Marilyn Monroe and Joe DiMaggio's in 1954. In 2004, hundreds of same-sex couples made the headlines by taking their vows here (though later the marriages were legally invalidated).

Grace Cathedral *Neo-Gothic grandeur* `1 D5`
1100 California Street • 415 749 6300 (events line 415 749 6350)
» www.gracecathedral.org Open 7–6 Mon–Fri, 8–6 Sat, 7–7 Sun, 8–4 church holidays

Grace, the country's third-largest Episcopal cathedral, is built in a French Gothic style with a lovely rose window and a monumental organ with carved oak screens. The front doors are cast copies of Ghiberti's Doors of Paradise in Florence's Baptistry.

Established Art Galleries
All the long-established and well-respected galleries are downtown and easy to find (Map 4 E1 & F1). **Fraenkel Gallery** (49 Geary St., www.fraenkelgallery.com) presents high-profile shows and represents most of the big names in photography. In the same building, **Stephen Wirtz Gallery** (www.wirtzgallery.com) deals mainly in conceptual art and photography. **Gallery Paule Anglim** (14 Geary St., www.gallerypauleanglim.com) showcases paintings, sculpture, and conceptual art. American postwar and younger contemporary artists are the focus at **John Berggruen Gallery** (228 Grant Ave., www.berggruen.com), while **Modernism** (685 Market St., www.modernisminc.com) primarily deals in early-20th-century international avant-garde painters.

Art & Architecture

Victorian Architecture *painted ladies*

San Francisco is justly famous for its Victorian architecture. It's one of the city's most visible styles, with some 15,000 Victorian homes still remaining. The best examples can be found in Pacific Heights, Presidio Heights, and on Alamo Square (all Map 8), but you'll also come across them in the Mission (Map 5) and Lower Haight (Map 10, *see p131*).

Most of these Victorian homes were built in the latter half of the 1800s, typically of wood with elaborate decorative elements, and most fall into one of four styles. Gothic Revival is characterized by steep gables and pointed windows with decorative vergeboards. Go to 1111 Oak Street (Map 10 G2) to see one of the city's oldest buildings in this style. The Italianate style is recognizable for its flat roofs, tall bracketed cornices, and angled bay windows; a typical example is 1913 Sacramento Street (Map 1 A5). In Stick-style houses (sometimes called Eastlake), bay windows are square or rectangular (not angled), and decorative gables are incorporated, often with a sunburst design, as at 1715–1717 Capp Street (Map 5 C5). The Queen Anne style is typified by gabled roofs, angled bay windows, and turrets; see 850 Steiner Street (Map 8 H5).

The best way to get to know more is by taking a tour, and there are several excellent options. **The Pacific Heights Walking Tour** (415 441 3004, www.sfheritage.org) is based at the Haas-Lilienthal House, 2007 Franklin Street (Map 1 B5). **The Victorian Home Walk** (415 252 9485, www.victorianwalk.com) begins by meeting downtown and proceeds to Pacific Heights, Western Addition, and Cow Hollow. **San Francisco City Guides** (415 557 4266, www.sfcityguides.org) offers three different tours with a Victorian focus. **A Friend In Town** (800 960 8099, www.toursan franciscobay.com) provides customized van tours.

Fort Mason Center *cultural collective* `1 A2`

Marina Boulevard at Buchanan Street • 415 441 3400

>> www.fortmason.org Check website for opening times

This former army base is home to many cultural organizations. The **SFMOMA Artists Gallery** (www.sfmoma.org) offers a rent-with-option-to-buy program and represents northern California artists, while Italian and Italian-American art is on show at **The Museo Italo-Americano** (www.museoitaloamericano.org). **Adm**

Coit Tower *iconic monument with panoramic views* `2 E3`

1 Telegraph Hill Boulevard • 415 362 0808

Open 10–6 daily

This distinctive city icon atop Telegraph Hill was erected in 1933 as a memorial, both to its benefactress – eccentric socialite heiress Lillie Coit – and to the city's firemen. Its lobbies are adorned with New Deal fresco murals commissioned by the Public Works of Art Project, a precurser to the Works Progress Administration's Federal Arts Project. Admission to the mural gallery is free, but it costs $3.75 to ride the tower elevator.

Palace of Fine Arts *romantic ruin* `8 F2`

3301 Lyon Street • 415 563 6504 (theater box office)

>> www.exploratorium.edu

This San Francisco Beaux-Arts icon was built by Bay Area Arts and Crafts architect Bernard Maybeck for the city's 1915 Panama-Pacific International Exposition. The original structure was temporary – made of chicken wire and stucco – and fell into a state of disrepair until it was finally rebuilt of lasting materials in the 1960s. Conceived as a Roman ruin in the style of a Piranesi engraving, the palace was meant to set a contemplative tone for visitors coming to the adjacent exhibition hall, which housed the work of then-living artists, predominantly Impressionists.

Today, it's a lovely site for a picnic or just for a stroll along the pond, among the "ruins." It's especially romantic in the evenings, when it's dramatically lit. The former exhibition hall now houses the Palace of Fine Arts Theater and the interactive Exploratorium science museum devoted to human perception.

>> *For more on painted ladies, see www.paintedladies.com*

Art & Architecture

Cartoon Art Museum *funny business* `4 F1`
655 Mission Street • 415 227 8666
>> www.cartoonart.org Open 11–5 Tue–Sun

The only museum of its kind in the US, the Cartoon Art Museum was established in 1987 with an endowment from *Peanuts* creator Charles M. Schulz. Although it's a smallish collection, it offers a rare glimpse into the creation of this neglected art. There's also an onsite bookstore and research library. **Adm**

Museum of Craft and Folk Art `4 E2`
51 Yerba Buena Lane • 415 227 4888
>> www.mocfa.org Open 11–6 Tue–Fri, 11–5 Sat & Sun

This Yerba Buena Gardens-based museum is known for its innovative and diverse exhibitions of local and international contemporary craft and folk art. Shows range in subject matter from African-American quiltmaking to Scandinavian modernists' influence on contemporary California design. **Adm**

Crown Point Press *renowned printmaker* `4 F2`
20 Hawthorne Street • 415 974 6273
>> www.crownpoint.com Open 10–6 Tue–Sat

Opened in 1962 as a printmaking workshop, this internationally known printer and publisher of printworks is credited with helping to revive the etching as a serious art form. The gallery exhibits etchings from invited artists. There's an in-house bookstore, and printmaking workshops in summer.

Multi-Museum Passes

To pack a number of museums into a short visit, get a multi-pass. **City Pass** (www.citypass.com) gets you in to SFMOMA *(see p78)*, the Legion of Honor *(see pp80–81)*, the Asian Art Museum *(see p70)*, and throws in a MUNI/cable car pass. The **Go SF Card** (www.gosanfranciscocard.com) also covers most of the smaller museums and historical sites.

Yerba Buena Center for the Arts `4 F2`
701 Mission Street • 415 978 2787
>> www.ybca.org Open noon–5 Tue–Sun (to 8 Thu)

Known as a venue for "adventurous" art, this well-respected center presents visual and performing arts programs in several venues. The gallery, just one component of the center, has no permanent collection. Instead, it curates temporary shows of mostly edgy modern art. **Adm**

Precita Eyes Mural Arts and Visitors Center *outdoor art tours*

`5 D4`

2981 24th Street • 415 285 2287

>> www.precitaeyes.org Open 10–9 Mon & Thu, 10–5 Tue, Wed & Fri, 10–4 Sat, noon–4 Sun

The Precita Eyes Center offers guided walks and bike tours through the Mission District, an area famous for its hundreds of public murals along Balmy and Clarion alleys, and on the Women's Building on 18th Street.

Mission Dolores *the city's oldest building*

`5 A2`

3321 16th Street • 415 621 8203

>> www.missiondolores.org Open 9–4 daily

This adobe church dates from 1776, when San Francisco was called Yerba Buena. The sixth of 21 missions ordered by King Carlos III of Spain to be established along a route stretching from Mexico to Sonoma, CA, it was actually built by converted Ohlone Indians. Docent tours are conducted for a modest fee. **Adm**

New Langton Arts *nonprofit art space*

`3 D4`

1246 Folsom Street • 415 626 5416

>> www.newlangtonarts.org Open noon–6 Tue–Sat

This alternative gallery is a home to visual art, spoken word, theater, and music, presented in its gallery space, screening room, and black box theater. You might see a performance piece, a mixed-media installation show, a piece of light-art in the front window "mini-gallery," or surf their online collection of cyberart pieces.

Alternative Galleries

Collecting art isn't just for old fogies and it doesn't have to cost a fortune, as these galleries prove. **Hang** (Map 3 D1, 556 & 567 Sutter St., www.hangart.com) makes fresh local art accessible and shopping for it fun, with special events and an additional online gallery. In the Mission, **Southern Exposure** (Map 5 D2, 401 Alabama St., www.soex. org) is a nonprofit artist-run organization presenting cutting-edge art in a lofty and spacious setting. Part gallery, part café, **The Canvas** (Map 9 D3, 1200 9th Ave., www.thecanvasgallery.com) offers works from emerging artists plus happening nightly activities, and the **Thomas Reynolds Gallery** (Map 8 H4, 2291 Pine St., www.thomasreynolds. com) specializes in California Realism.

Art & Architecture

San Francisco Museum of Modern Art 4 F2
renowned international art collection
151 3rd Street • 415 357 4000
>> www.sfmoma.org Open 11–5:45 Fri–Tue, 11–8:45 Thu

Swiss architect Mario Botta's striking modernist building made a splash when it opened in 1995, and it's looking even better these days, surrounded by new highrises and with the matured Yerba Buena Gardens *(see p143)* at its doorstep.

SFMOMA was the first museum on the West Coast devoted to modern art, and it's still the second-largest modern art museum building in the country. The collection includes important Abstract Expressionists, Bay Area and Southern California artists, photographers, and media artists, and the museum frequently presents or hosts terrific special exhibitions. Visitors tend to make a beeline for the MuseumStore *(see p59)*, which houses one of the West Coast's best collections of art books, and the café, a pleasant place to while away a sunny afternoon. **Adm**

Cantor Arts Center *Rodin riches*
328 Lomita Drive, Stanford • 650 723 4177 • Take San Jose-bound train to Palo Alto, then bus No. 280 to Arboretum Rd.
>> museum.stanford.edu Open 11–5 Wed–Sun (to 8 Thu)

Among other significant holdings, this handsome museum at Stanford University boasts the largest collection of Rodin's bronzes outside Paris, including *The Monument to Balzac* and *The Gates of Hell*. The *Burghers of Calais* can be seen on the campus grounds.

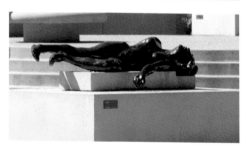

Memorial Church *Byzantine-style splendor*
Stanford University • San Jose-bound train to Palo Alto, then University shuttle bus or Samtrans bus No. 280 to Arboretum Rd.
>> stanford.edu/group/religiouslife
Open 8–5 Mon–Fri; services 10am Sun

This 1903 nondenominational church at the heart of the Stanford campus is one of the most splendid buildings in the country, with stunning large-scale mosaics and exquisite stained-glass windows.

de Young Museum *art of the Americas* 9 C2

Golden Gate Park, 50 Hagiwara Tea Garden Dr. • 415 750 3600
>> www.thinker.org/deyoung Open 9:30–5 Tue–Sun (to 8:45 Fri)

Reopened in 2005, the new de Young, designed by Swiss architects Herzog & de Meuron (responsible for London's Tate Modern), is the city's most controversial building in decades. Say what you will about the structure's swooping asymmetry, its dramatic embossed and perforated copper cladding (designed to fade to verdigris in time), and its twisting parallelogram of a tower, it gives a jolt of energy to a once-staid setting. And its new site-specific works by Andy Goldsworthy, Gerhard Richter, and James Turrell, are exceptional.

The museum itself specializes in American paintings, decorative arts, and sculpture from the 17th century to the present; native arts from the Americas, the Pacific Islands, and Africa; and textiles from many areas and ages. Its Rockefeller Collection of American Paintings is the foremost of its kind in the West. **Adm**

Neptune Society Columbarium 8 E5

1 Loraine Court • 415 771 0717
Open 8–5 Mon–Fri, 10–2 Sat & Sun

This 1898 Neo-Baroque jewel box is the final resting place for the ashes of thousands of early (and some more recent) San Franciscans, including historic city figures. Abandoned between 1934 and 1979, the building has been restored to its former glory and features fantastic stained glass and artwork.

Museum Cafés

Dining at museums used to be a dismal affair, but count on food-crazy San Franciscans to raise the bar significantly. The major art museums all now have cafés worthy of a visit in their own right. The **de Young Café** *(see above)*, which looks out at the sculpture garden, offers tempting seasonal dishes created from local artisinal ingredients. Café Asia, at the **Asian Art Museum** *(see p70)*, offers Oriental-inspired surprises like Tibetan lamb stew or green tea soba noodles. Over at the **Legion of Honor Café** *(see pp80–1)*, you might enjoy fancy tea sandwiches or grilled flank steak, while at **SFMOMA**'s Caffè Museo *(see p78)*, the menu is Mediterranean. All four places also offer dining spaces outdoors for when the weather is fine.

Legion of Honor

Lincoln Park, 34th Avenue and Clement Street • 415 863 3330
» www.thinker.org/legion Open 9:30–5 Tue–Sun

This gem at Land's End is a perfect art museum – small and easily viewed, but satisfyingly varied and exceptionally beautiful. Spending an afternoon here is like taking a little vacation without leaving the city.

The Legion of Honor is sister to the de Young museum, and together they comprise the Fine Arts Museums of San Francisco, one of the largest art museum entities in the US. The site, immortalized in Hitchcock's *Vertigo* and later in Armistead Maupin's book *Tales of the City*, has the kind of picture-postcard views that people travel from around the world to see. Lincoln Park is spread out at the museum's doorstep, and the land slopes down to reveal vistas of the Golden Gate, the bridge, and the Marin Headlands. Amid pine and eucalyptus trees, and surrounded by hiking trails, a beach, and a golf course, it's an incomparable setting for a museum.

The building itself is a three-quarter scale adaptation of the Palais de la Légion d'Honneur in Paris, and just walking into the grand entry plaza makes you wonder if you will need euros to buy a ticket. The solemn air of its Neoclassical colonnades is fitting, since it was built to honor the 3,600 California residents who died in battle in France during World War I. Designed by architect George Applegarth and opened on Armistice Day 1924, the building underwent a huge retrofit and renovation from 1992 to 1995, which included seismic strengthening and added two lower levels underground.

Inside the museum, the collection's primary focus is on European painting and decorative art. Most notable is a splendid collection of some 80 Rodin sculptures, many of which were personally selected at Rodin's studio before his death in 1917 by Alma de Bretteville Spreckels, the museum's Francophile founder. Also especially noteworthy is the Achenbach Foundation for Graphic Arts collection, one of the largest collections of prints, drawings, and illustrated books in the US. The vast collection includes more than 70,000 works dating from the late 15th century to the present, and features Old Master prints and drawings, Japanese prints, Persian and Indian miniatures, 19th-century photography, modern and contemporary graphics, and artists' books. The museum also has a Theater and Dance Collection, which is one of the country's foremost repositories of theatrical costume and set design.

The galleries on the main floor are arranged chronologically and to some extent by country or area. They feature a wealth of masterpieces from artists like Fra Angelico, El Greco, Tintoretto, Gainsborough, Reynolds, Constable, Rembrandt, Rubens, Van Dyck, Goya, and many more; and wandering among the airy, spacious rooms is a pleasure. One gallery presents a smallish but charming collection of Impressionist and Post-Impressionist paintings.

Downstairs, in the new lower levels, there are more galleries (including one for special exhibits), a theater, and a small museum shop. A visit can be completed by a leisurely lunch or afternoon tea on the lovely garden terrace of the café, and if you want to extend your visit after you've returned home, the museum's website has a "virtual gallery," which allows you to choose from among 82,000 works of art to create your own galleries in cyberspace. **Adm**

Art & Architecture

The Beach Chalet *murals and mosaics* `11 A4`
1000 Great Highway • 415 386 8439
>> www.beachchalet.com Open 9am–midnight daily

Architect Willis Polk was a protégé of Chicago's Daniel
Burnham and helped him with San Francisco's master
plan. He also designed this 1925 beachfront building,
which contains interesting 1930s Works Progress
Administration (WPA) fresco murals, mosaics, and
carvings, as well as a café and restaurant *(see p145)*.

Berkeley Art Museum *East Bay treasure*
2626 Bancroft Way, Berkeley • 510 642 0808 • BART Richmond
Line to downtown Berkeley, then a short walk across campus
>> www.bampfa.berkeley.edu Open 11–5 Wed–Sun (to 7 Thu)

This modernist building houses a broad collection of
artworks, with a focus on 20th-century pieces. Founded
in 1963 with the donation of 45 paintings by Hans
Hofmann, the museum now boasts some 14,000
objects, from Old Masters to conceptual works. **Adm**

Paramount Theatre *Art Deco movie palace*
2025 Broadway, Oakland • 510 465 6400 • Any East Bay-
bound BART line to 19th St. in downtown Oakland
>> www.paramounttheatre.com Tours given at 10am on the
1st and 3rd Sat of the month; private tours arranged for a fee

The last great movie palace to be built, and one of only
a few still standing, is rivaled in splendor only by New
York's Radio City Music Hall. Completed in 1931 and
painstakingly restored in 1973, it is now listed as a
National Historic Landmark. The Art Deco-style theater
is especially noted for its stylistic harmony –
incorporating detailed metalwork and tiling, murals,
fabrics, sculptures, and reliefs into one seamless whole.
From the huge oversize mosaic on the exterior façade,
through to the grand lobby with its "fountain of light,"
and into the magnificent main hall with its spectacular
grillwork ceiling, the effect is continually dazzling. The
theater is home to the Oakland East Bay Symphony
and the Oakland Ballet. Touring musicians often appear
and classic movies are screened on Fridays. **Adm**

Chapel of the Chimes and Mountain View Cemetery *at rest in Oakland*

Chapel: 4499 Piedmont Avenue, Oakland • 510 654 0123
>> www.chapelofthechimes.com Open 9–5 daily
Cemetery: 5000 Piedmont Avenue, Oakland • 510 658 2588
>> www.mountainviewcemetery.org Open 7am–sunset daily
Take any East Bay-bound BART line to MacArthur station, then
AC transit bus No. 57 to 40th and Broadway, then short walk

Cemeteries and columbaria don't top most people's "to do" lists, but these two spots in the Oakland foothills make a surprisingly enjoyable outing.

The lovely Chapel of the Chimes columbarium was principally designed by architect Julia Morgan, who also designed William Randolph Hearst's famous "castle," and was the first woman to graduate in architecture from the École des Beaux-Arts in Paris. The columbarium is one of her masterworks, a rambling series of cloisters, chapels, courtyards, and alcoves, filled with beautiful stained glass, paintings, mosaics, statues, gardens, and fountains.

Designed in an Arts and Crafts amalgam of Romanesque and Gothic styles, the spaces vary in size and scale and are arranged on several levels. The massing and progression of these unique spaces has a rhythm and vitality that, together with the beautiful decorative elements, dispel the air of death – it's peaceful and not at all creepy. The containers of remains (many shaped like thick books) are fascinating to browse and give the sense more of being in a splendid library than a mausoleum. Decorative treasures include ancient hand-illuminated hymn books and a Della Robbia plaque.

Next door, the handsome Mountain View Cemetery also has a distinguished design pedigree, its curving lanes and grand boulevards having been laid out in 1863 by Frederick Law Olmsted, creator of New York's Central Park. The monuments and graves range in style from Egyptian and Greek Revival, to Arts and Crafts and Modern, and nestle among native live oaks, imported Italian stone pines, and palm trees.

performance

Ever since the days when it was a decadent Barbary Coast town, the residents of San Francisco have enjoyed their entertainment. Today, the city boasts a lively arts and cultural life that includes innovative, world-class symphony, opera, and ballet; cutting-edge music and performance art; and prize-winning poetry and literature. It also has some first-rate venues, from cozy supper clubs to grand theaters.

PERFORMANCE

One of the best things about going out in this town is the richness of choice, not just in the variety of its offerings but also in the splendor of its venues. Whether you're a fan of jazz, rock, or classical music, comedy, theater, or dance, chances are you'll find something to love, and you'll see it in a thrilling setting – up close, in an Art Deco palace, a retro nightclub, a jazz boîte that serves sushi, a funky black-box theater, or a bejeweled music hall.

Peter Cieply

Superlative Performance

The city's reputation has grown exponentially thanks to its high-culture trio: the **San Francisco Symphony, San Francisco Opera,** and **San Francisco Ballet** *(see pp92–3)* are all now recognized globally as being top-tier. In addition, **Cal Performances** *(see p98)* and **San Francisco Performances** *(see p88)* boast impressive rosters of international artists.

From Comedy to Vaudeville

How do you like your comedy – straight, or with a twist? Classic stand-up is on nightly at the **Punch Line** *(see p89)*, where famous comics have cut their teeth for decades. **Beach Blanket Babylon** *(see p89)* offers a camp take on current events, while **Teatro ZinZanni** *(see p91)* is a crazy vaudeville circus where you're served a gourmet dinner, too.

Unique Movie Houses

Alternatives to the multiplex experience can be found at the **Castro Theatre** *(see p96)*, a classic rep house that's a neighborhood icon, and at the **Red Vic Movie House** *(see p96)*, which features sofas to sit on and popcorn served in bowls. The funky **Parkway Speakeasy Theater** *(see p99)* goes one step further and sells food, beer, and wine.

choice acts

Edgy Alternatives

San Francisco prides itself on swimming outside the mainstream, and these venues follow suit. **Audium** *(see p94)*, the world's only "theater of sound," plays trippy soundscapes in a darkened room, while **The Marsh** *(see p97)* is a hothouse for solo performers. The eclectic **Intersection for the Arts** *(see p97)* showcases new music, theater, and visual art.

Jazz and Blues

Once considered the "Harlem of the West," San Francisco still takes jazz and blues seriously. Swell options for the former include **Yoshi's** *(see p99)*, a perfect venue with great sushi for added appeal, and **Jazz at Pearl's** *(see p88)*, a supper club with a terrific house *chanteuse* and band. For blues, the **Boom Boom Room** *(see p95)* is the place to be.

Gig Venues

It's hard to beat a great concert in a classic club. Former bordello the **Great American Music Hall** *(see p91)* juxtaposes indie rockers with its ornate interior, while **Bimbo's 365 Club** *(see p89)* showcases alt-rock and pop artists in a swanky 50s ballroom. **The Fillmore** *(see p95)* is legendary and worth taking in, almost regardless of who's playing.

Performance

San Francisco Performances

Various venues; for details and tickets call 415 398 6449
>> www.performances.org Box office open 9:30–5 Mon–Fri

For 25 years this organization has been bringing the highest caliber of musicians and dancers to San Francisco from around the world. Among these are emerging and established artists, ranging from pianists Evgeny Kissin and Lang Lang, to percussionist Evelyn Glennie, composer Philip Glass, and ballet choreographer Angelin Preljocaj. The Paul Taylor Dance Company is annually in residence for two weeks in the spring. A typical season might include a number of programs – a capella, dance, guitar, jazz, and piano virtuosi – and this diversity of programming attracts a wide spectrum of arts lovers.

Performances are held at a number of venues in the city and the East Bay – from small churches to huge concert halls like the Masonic Auditorium and Davies Symphony Hall *(see p92)*. There is also an intimate "musical salon" series at the Hotel Rex *(see p154)*.

Jazz at Pearl's *world-class jazz* `2 E4`
256 Columbus Avenue • 415 291 8255
>> www.jazzatpearls.com Shows 8pm and 10pm Thu–Mon

This intimate club has an in-house big band and its own diva – jazz and blues vocalist (and co-owner) Kim Nalley. While it bills itself as a supper club, it only serves cold tapas but offers meal deals at nearby restaurants if you reserve in advance. Do this too if you don't want to stand – there are just 25 tables.

Ticket Services

Tickets to concerts and sporting events are often handled by major ticketing agencies, which add hefty service charges. You can sometimes avoid these fees by purchasing directly from the box office; check individual venues. Otherwise, **Ticketmaster** (415 421 8497, www.ticketmaster.com) is the largest distributor and controls many venues. It has outlets in several of the city's **Tower Records** (www.towerrecords.com) and **Wherehouse** (www.wherehouse.com) stores. Cultural events and smaller venues tend to be handled by **Tickets.com** (800 225 2277, www.tickets.com), while **Tix Bay Area** (415 433 7827, www.tixbay area.com) sells half-price day-of-event tickets online and from a booth in Union Square and is a Ticketmaster outlet.

Bimbo's 365 Club *swank room for rockers* `1 C2`

1025 Columbus Avenue • 415 474 0365
>> www.bimbos365club.com Box office open 10–4 Mon–Fri

The swellest of the city's music venues, Bimbo's is a perfectly preserved 1950s nightclub that transports you back to the world of the Rat Pack. Seating is cabaret-style, the bartenders wear short white jackets, and there are bathroom attendants who will hand you towels and offer cologne. There's a clubby bar and lounge with a fireplace separate from the main room, and for some shows there's even a dance floor.

Ensconced in a booth or seated at one of the cocktail tables, you can almost hear Sinatra crooning from the red velvet-draped stage. Nowadays the lineup is mostly lesser-known alt-rock and pop artists, although occasionally heavy-hitters like Elvis Costello, Macy Gray, Chris Isaak, or The Strokes make a rare small-club appearance. Seating is not reserved, so arrive early for the best tables. There's a two-drink minimum in addition to the ticket cost.

Punch Line Comedy Club *for laughs* `2 F4`

444 Battery Street • 415 397 7573
>> www.punchlinecomedyclub.com Shows nightly

For 25 years Punch Line has been a training ground for comics, including the likes of Robin Williams, Ellen DeGeneres, and Chris Rock. It still draws big-name talent and fosters exciting up-and-comers. With parquet floors and wooden chairs, the club is small and comfy, and offers cocktails and light meals with the show.

Beach Blanket Babylon *camp cabaret* `1 D3`

Club Fugazi, 678 Green Street • 415 421 4222
>> www.beachblanketbabylon.com
Box office open 10–6 Mon–Sun

Beach Blanket Babylon is a San Francisco institution, and America's longest-running revue. It's a silly musical-comedy send-up of pop culture that changes with the zeitgeist. Nothing is sacred, and the only constant is the outrageously large hats.

Performance

American Conservatory Theater `3 D1`
415 Geary Street • 415 749 2228
>> www.act-sf.org Box office noon–6 (curtain time show days)

ACT is the city's major mainstream theater company and training conservatory, housed in the beautifully restored 1910 Geary Theater, a sleek blend of Neo-Baroque, Neoclassic, and contemporary styles. Shows range from the classics to new commissions and collaborative productions with other regional theaters.

Empire Plush Room *music and comedy* `3 C1`
York Hotel, 940 Sutter Street • 415 885 2800
>> www.plushroom.com/plushroom.htm
Box office open 3–7 Mon, noon–7 Tue–Sat

During Prohibition this jewel box of a venue was a speakeasy, accessed through a warren of tunnels. Today it's a welcoming lounge where you can hear an array of cabaret and jazz performers as well as comics like Sandra Bernhard and Joan Rivers.

Companies to Look Out For

There are a number of knockout dance and theater companies based in San Francisco which have either no regular home or no predictable season. Watch for these troupes performing around town, and catch them if you can.

LINES Ballet (415 863 3040, www.linesballet.org) is Alonzo King's innovative, award-winning contemporary classical dance company. **Smuin Ballet** (415 495 2234, www.smuinballet.org) showcases Michael Smuin's engaging mix of styles – a former principal dancer and choreographer for American Ballet Theatre, Smuin is also a Tony Award-winner and choreographed fights for the film *Star Wars: Episode II*, so he knows about pleasing a crowd. **Robert Moses' Kin** (415 252 8384, www.robert moseskin.org) performs works that range from ballet to postmodern dance and movement theater, often exploring issues of race, class, and gender;

while the **Joe Goode Performance Group** (415 561 6565, www.joegoode.org) crafts evocative dance-theater pieces that combine Goode's physical, high-velocity choreography with spoken texts and singing.

Consistently one of the strongest small companies in town, the **Encore Theatre Company** (415 821 4849, www.encoretheatrecompany.org) produces mostly new works in intimate stagings. **42nd Street Moon** (415 978 2787, www.42ndstmoon.org) puts the spotlight on musicals, and is one of the world's oldest companies devoted to staging concert performances of "lost" works (the Gershwin brothers' *Funny Face*, Cole Porter's *Can-Can*, etc.). For smart and funny sketch comedy, look out for **Killing My Lobster** (415 558 7721, www.killingmylobster.com), a troupe whose cast changes frequently, but whose humor remains killing. Every year they produce an imaginative high-concept/low-budget film festival which then tours nationwide.

Great American Music Hall `3 C2`
859 O'Farrell Street • 415 885 0750
>> www.musichallsf.com Box office open 10:30–6 Mon–Fri
(to 9pm show nights), to 1 hr before shows Sat & Sun

This sumptuous Rococo hall is San Francisco's oldest nightclub. These days it's a live music venue, playing host to indie rockers and big name pop acts. You can dance beneath the frescoes and marble columns on the first floor, or order a burger and a drink upstairs.

The Warfield *rock and pop hall* `3 D2`
982 Market Street
415 775 7722

This 1922 former vaudeville theater has been converted into a terrific midsize music venue, hosting mostly pop and rock artists. Amid Art Deco splendor, there's a standing area up front, table seating with food and drink service on the main level, and some reserved seating in the balcony.

Teatro ZinZanni *zany circus and dinner* `2 F2`
Pier 29, The Embarcadero • 415 438 2668
>> love.zinzanni.org Box office open 10–6 daily

Teatro ZinZanni's subtitle "Love, Chaos, and Dinner" doesn't really explain what to expect, but then, it is difficult to describe. The term "dinner theater" is too bourgeois, and "cabaret" doesn't really capture it. Its home is an early 1900s Belgian *spiegeltent* (mirror tent) pitched on the waterfront at Pier 29, with a lavishly appointed interior of burnished wood, beveled mirrors, and plush velvet upholstry. Inside, circus performers and a crafty kitchen keep audiences grinning through five courses. The changing cast of circus and vaudeville performers from around the world – illusionists, comics, contortionists, trapeze artists, jugglers, fire eaters, musicians, and singers – entertain patrons as they dine, occasionally hauling a few unsuspecting souls out of their comfy seats and into the spotlight for some audience participation (be forewarned if you're sitting near the center of the action).

Performance »»»»»

San Francisco War Memorial and Performing Arts Center 3 B3 *classical culture*

201–401 Van Ness Avenue • 415 621 6600
»» www.sfwmpac.org

The Performing Arts Center is right at the heart of the city's cultural life. From south to north along Van Ness Avenue, it comprises the Louise M. Davies Symphony Hall, the War Memorial Opera House, and the War Memorial Veterans Building (which houses the Herbst Theatre). The complex forms part of the city's grand Civic Center, and was designed in the 1920s to harmonize with the monumental Beaux Arts-style City Hall *(see p71)* across the street. Construction was finally completed in 1932.

The **San Francisco Symphony** (415 864 6000, www. sfsymphony.org), under the direction of music director Michael Tilson Thomas (or MTT as he's affectionately called), has become one of the world's finest and most adventurous orchestras, and it's a pleasure to hear

them at the Davies Symphony Hall. This very modern building was designed by Skidmore, Owings, and Merrill in 1980, and underwent a revamp of its acoustics in 1992. Now it's a stellar auditorium with vibrant rich sound, plush comfortable seats, and an open modern aesthetic. MTT is known for championing new and unfamiliar works, and he's a charismatic and dynamic conductor, throwing himself bodily into the music. He's also been known to address the audience, to explain a composer's intent or to help listeners understand particular juxtapositions in programming, so he's an entertaining educator as well.

The **San Francisco Opera** (415 864 3330, www.sf opera.com) is the second-largest opera company in the US, and has long been esteemed internationally. Like the symphony, in recent times it has been heralded for its adventurousness. The War Memorial Opera House in which the company performs is elegant and luxurious, having undergone an extensive renovation

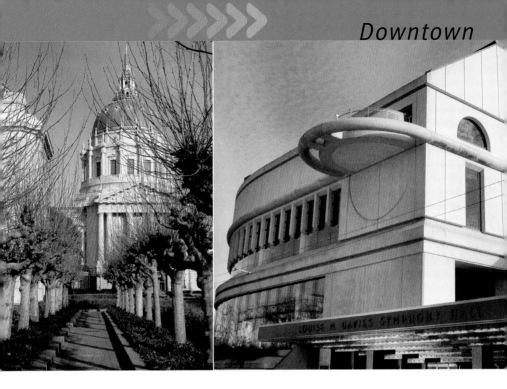

and retrofit in 1997. The acoustics, however, have been called spotty, and ironically some of the cheapest seats may actually be best in this regard – the upper balcony and standing room enjoy heavenly sound. If you're up to the challenge, 150 standing-room seats go on sale at 10am on the day of performance for only $10 (cash only, one per person).

Also housed in the War Memorial Opera House is the **San Francisco Ballet** (415 865 2000, www.sfballet.org). It is the nation's oldest ballet company, founded in 1933 as the San Francisco Opera Ballet and striking out on its own in 1942. The company was the first in America to present the complete *Nutcracker* ballet, which remains a holiday staple, now in a brand-new staging by artistic director Helgi Tomasson, who took over in 1985. Under his direction the ballet has risen from the ranks of regional companies to achieve world-class status and is noted for its rigorous classicism. Its repertory is

broad-ranging and ever-evolving and includes works from eminent choreographer George Balanchine, numerous pieces by Tomasson himself, and commissions from contemporary choreographers like Mark Morris. The Ballet also offers same-day standing-room tickets, available from 10am onward on the day of performance; price varies, based on the least-expensive seat price.

The **Herbst Theatre** (401 Van Ness Ave., 415 392 4400) in the War Memorial Veterans Building is a beautiful little gem of an auditorium, decorated with Beaux-Arts murals originally created for the 1915 Panama-Pacific International Exposition. The War Memorial complex served as the birthplace of the United Nations in 1945, and its charter was signed on this stage. Today the theater is used by various presenters for music performances and recitals, film and lecture series *(see p94)*, and the occasional theater or dance event.

Performance >>>>>

City Arts & Lectures *high-brow talks* 3 B3
Herbst Theatre, 401 Van Ness Avenue • 415 392 4400
>> www.cityarts.net

Dropping in on this lecture series leaves you feeling smart and sophisticated – how civilized to while away an evening in the company of a respected writer, artist, or thinker, interviewed live by a local luminary. Events take place in the beautiful Herbst Theatre *(see p93)*, making it even more of a pleasure.

Magic Theatre *new works playhouse* 1 A1
Building D, Fort Mason Center • 415 441 8001
>> www.magictheatre.org Box office open noon–5 Tue–Sat

The Magic is one of the nation's most prominent theaters dedicated to new works. It was Sam Shepard's first home, and both he and fellow playwright David Mamet have premiered works here. The theater's two performance spaces are housed in a lofty converted warehouse in the Fort Mason Center *(see p73)*.

Audium *otherwordly audio experience* 3 B1
1616 Bush Street • 415 771 1616
>> www.audium.org
Performances at 8:30pm Fri & Sat

The world's only "theater of sound" uses space as a compositional tool. The lights fade to darkness and the audience floats in a sea of sounds emanating from 169 speakers in the walls, floor, and ceiling. A dreamlike and quintessentially trippy SF experience.

Get the Spirit
Sunday mornings offer a couple of unique opportunities to get right with the Spirit while enjoying some devilishly good music. The **St. John Coltrane African Orthodox Church** (Map 8 H5, 1286 Fillmore St., www.coltranechurch.org) has canonized jazz saxophonist Coltrane and bases its services on his music, incorporating it into the Sunday noon liturgy and riffing righteously. **Glide Memorial United Methodist Church** (Map 3 D2, 330 Ellis St., www.glide.org) draws folks from around the globe (visitors have included Oprah and Bill Clinton) who come to hear the Good News, told gospel style – the choir and soloists raise the roof. It is worth noting that both these organizations also do tremendous social work for the hungry and homeless.

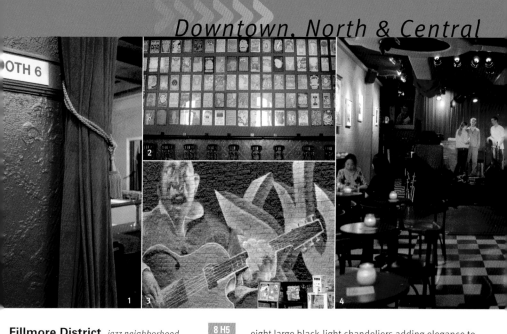

Fillmore District *jazz neighborhood* `8 H5`

Fillmore Street has long been a center for music. Historically an ethnically diverse neighborhood, the Fillmore became San Francisco's first major African American community during World War II. Dozens of jazz clubs opened and it became known as the "Harlem of the West." The area was fairly decimated with urban renewal projects in the 1950s and 60s, but now plans are being made for a new "jazz preservation district." Until then, the action is still centered around three established live music spots on the street.

At the junction with Geary Boulevard, **The Fillmore** theater (1805 Geary Blvd., 415 346 6000, www. thefillmore.com), built in 1912, is a midsize venue hosting acts from across the whole spectrum of popular music: rock, pop, blues, metal, folk, and more. It became a mecca for rock music during the 1960s. The careers of the Grateful Dead, Jefferson Airplane, Janis Joplin, and many others were launched from the stage of this beautiful old venue. These days, the quality and variety remains consistently excellent, and some of the biggest names in music can be heard here. The room is fairly intimate, with eight large black-light chandeliers adding elegance to the funky old ballroom. Crowds are consistently well behaved, and not just due to the reefer smoke wafting through this nonsmoking hall; people just enjoy being here. The main floor is standing room only, though there is some seating in the balcony.

Across Fillmore Street is **Rasselas on Fillmore Jazz Club** (No. 1534, 415 346 8696, www.rasselasjazz club.com), which offers jazz, R&B, and blues nightly. An unusual menu of Ethiopian food is served either in the adjoining restaurant or in the club itself, where much of the seating takes the form of plush sofas. In the bar area there's a cozy fireplace, small tables, several booths, and a full drinks menu. It's generally hip and happening, so arrive early to secure a seat.

On the other side of Geary Boulevard, you can boogie the night away at the **Boom Boom Room** (No. 1601, 415 673 8000, www.boomboomblues.com). This funky-chic joint is just what you want from a blues club: small, low-lit, and red-hot. Blues, New Orleans funk, groove, and soul music is live seven nights a week, and sometimes big name acts will drop by after their local sets and perform here.

Red Vic Movie House *funky rep cinema* `10 F2`
1727 Haight Street • 415 668 3994
»» www.redvicmoviehouse.com

If you're tired of sterile corporate movie houses, make yourself comfortable at this Haight-Ashbury art-house cinema. Owned and operated by a cooperative, it's as anti-corporate as they come. Seating options include comfy old sofas, and the concession-stand fare features organic snacks and bowls (not boxes) of popcorn.

Castro Theatre *iconic movie palace* `10 H3`
429 Castro Street • 415 621 6120
»» www.thecastrotheatre.com

This grand old dame is a splendid, though faded, Art Deco movie palace. Its marquee is an icon in this famous gay neighborhood, and the place really comes into its own with screenings of camp classics. It's a rare example of a great film repertory house, with broad-ranging programs and interesting series and festivals.

Theatre Rhinoceros *gay theater crucible* `5 C1`
2926 16th Street • 415 861 5079
»» www.therhino.org Box office open 1–6 Wed–Sun

America's longest-running professional queer theater makes its home in this comfy Mission space. There's a main stage and a small studio theater, and mostly gay and lesbian works are staged, including premieres from local favorites like comedian Marga Gomez, playwright John Fisher, and theater company Five Lesbian Brothers.

Going Out to the Ball Game
Sports fans here have twice the opportunity to get riled up, since San Francisco and Oakland both have pro teams. For baseball, besides the action at AT&T Park *(see opposite)*, you can take the BART across the Bay to catch the **Oakland A's** (www.oaklandathletics.com) in their games at McAfee Coliseum. Football fans will find the **San Francisco 49ers** (www.49ers.com) at their home, Monster Park. The city operates special buses to all home games. For football in Oakland, call on the **Raiders** (www.raiders.com), also at home in the McAfee Coliseum, while for basketball, see the **Golden State Warriors** (510 986 2200, www.warriors.com) at the Arena in Oakland. Tickets to games are sold through the major ticketing agencies *(see p88)*.

The Marsh *solo-performers' proving ground* `5 B4`
1062 Valencia Street • 415 826 5750
>> www.themarsh.org

This funky Mission venue is a greenhouse for solo performers. There's usually a strong solo show on offer in the tiny theater, with a Monday Night Marsh series for works-in-progress, and the Mock Café, a Saturday night stand-up comedy series. They also offer classes on creating and performing your own work.

Intersection for the Arts *arts space* `5 B1`
446 Valencia Street • 415 626 3311
>> www.theintersection.org

SF's oldest alternative arts space presents new works of literature, theater, music, and the visual arts. It is also home to Campo Santo, a respected small theater company whose work focuses on storytelling. Come here to browse the galleries, hear some jazz, catch a new performance piece, or just see great theater.

Yerba Buena Center for the Arts `4 F2`
700 Howard Street • 415 978 2787
>> www.ybca.org

This striking arts campus presents bold art in many formats *(see p74)*, including theater and film. Artists who've worked here range from the acclaimed director Peter Sellars to film-maker Miranda July and DJ Spooky, and film series range from the Jewish film festival to screenings by Human Rights Watch.

AT&T Park *baseball by the Bay* `4 H3`
24 Willie Mays Plaza • 415 972 2000
>> www.sfgiants.com
Ticket office 8:30–5:30 Mon–Fri & during all Giants home games

Enjoy the great American pastime at this baseball stadium, which offers some of the best views of any park – not just of Barry Bonds and the Giants, who are great to watch, but also of the Bay, glittering just beyond the scoreboard (if it's not socked in with fog).

>> *Theatre Bay Area (www.theatrebayarea.org) has comprehensive listings of what's on*

Cal Performances *best bet for culture-vultures*

Zellerbach Hall, UC Berkeley • 510 642 9988 • BART to Downtown
Berkeley Station, then walk east to the university campus
» www.calperfs.berkeley.edu
Box office 10–5:30 Tue–Fri, 1–5 Sat & Sun

Cal Performances might be one of the best things that
ever happened to the Bay Area performing arts scene,
which can tend toward provincialism. The organization
is the performing arts presenter for the University of
California, in Berkeley, and it imports some of the best
performers and groups from around the globe. Both
established and emerging artists are featured, from
the worlds of classical, chamber, jazz and world music;
classical and modern dance; theater and spoken word.
It also commissions new works (it is a second home
to choreographer Mark Morris, who often premieres
works here) and hosts a biennial early music festival.

There's something for everyone. Acts in recent
times have included Ladysmith Black Mambazo,
mezzo-soprano Cecilia Bartoli, Russia's legendary
Kirov Ballet and Orchestra, the National Ballet of
China, modern jazz pianist Brad Mehldav and jazz
guitarist Bill Frisell, the Alvin Ailey American
Dance Theater, and the Dave Brubeck Quartet
and Ramsey Lewis Trio.

The majority of performances take place on campus
in the cavernous Zellerbach Hall, a nonetheless
comfortable auditorium with great sightlines, and
Hertz Hall, a smaller auditorium with better acoustics.
Theater performances are given in the intimate
Zellerbach Playhouse. All venues are easily accessed
from San Francisco via BART, and restaurant and bar
options abound nearby in downtown Berkeley or
along the funkier Telegraph Avenue strip *(see p135)*.

Berkeley Repertory Theatre *fresh new drama*
2025 Addison St., Berkeley • 510 647 2949 • BART to
Downtown Berkeley Station, then a short walk to Addison St.
➤➤ www.berkeleyrep.org Box office noon–7 Tue–Sun

Founded in 1968 as the East Bay's first professional
theater company, Berkeley Rep has become an
important regional theater, offering fresh takes on
classics and new works. Younger patrons should take
advantage of the unusual "under-30" discount.

Parkway Speakeasy Theater *pizza & film*
1834 Park Blvd., Oakland • 510 814 2400 • BART to Lake
Merritt Station, then take bus No. 40 to 12th St. and Oak St.
➤➤ www.picturepubpizza.com

Dinner-and-a-movie has never been so easy, cheap,
and cheerful. Order at the concession stand, and
when the food is ready, servers bring it to your
comfy sofa or cocktail table in the funky theater.
Screenings range from recent hits to cult classics.

Shotgun Players *plucky theater group*
1901 Ashby Ave., Berkeley • 510 841 6500 • BART to Ashby Stn.
➤➤ www.shotgunplayers.org

For almost 15 years this interesting and intrepid
ensemble has been staging everything from Greek
tragedies to works by Camus, Dylan Thomas, and
local favorite Adam Bock, and doing it everywhere
from pizza parlors to prisons. They finally got their
own space in 2004, in a converted former church.

Yoshi's *jazz and sushi joint*
510 Embarcadero West, Oakland • 510 238 9200 • BART to
W. Oakland Station, then bus No. 62 to 5th Ave. and E. 10th St.
➤➤ www.yoshis.com Box office 10am–10:30pm daily

This intimate club is a favorite gig for many jazz
musicians, and audiences groove on it too. The stage
is equipped with a top-flight custom Meyer Sound
system, a Steinway Concert D grand piano, and state-
of-the-art lighting, and there isn't a bad seat in the
house. There is a twice-nightly, 363-day-a-year (closed
Thanksgiving and Christmas) lineup of musicians
drawn from the top ranks of the jazz world, from
pianists Oscar Peterson and McCoy Tyner, to singers
Dianne Reeves and Diana Krall, and even Woody Allen.
    Yoshi's serves not just cocktails but also sushi and
Japanese food, and you can dine either in the
adjoining restaurant or in the club itself. What more
could a jazz fan ask? Note that if you dine in the
restaurant before the late show, they'll reserve a
table for you, otherwise it's open seating.

The Pacific Film Archive is a film institute which shares a building with the Berkeley Art Museum (see p82)

bars & clubs

San Francisco is the most bibulous city in North America west of the Mississippi, and a party destination for people who come from far and wide for a weekend in "The City." From high-tech dance clubs and elegant cocktail lounges to dark dive bars and characterful saloons, here you'll find the best of both high and low in which to lift a glass.

BARS & CLUBS

San Francisco may have a healthy reputation, but it's no stranger to hedonism. Those looking for world-renowned DJs, mango mojitos, or the Prada-clad crowd won't be let down. The gay scene is just as vibrant as ever, as is the music scene: with plenty of jazz, swing, rock, and hard-to-classify shows. And if all you want is a pint and a bite, both bargain and decadent fare is available. So eat, drink, and be merry – at least until the (inexplicably early) 2am last call.

Heather Wagner

And The Beat Goes On

In the South of Market area, DJs favoring house, funk, and classic drum and bass spin nightly to gyrating crowds at effervescent clubs such as **Mezzanine** *(see p115)* and **Duplex** *(see p119)*. While you might find yourself languishing outside the velvet rope – especially at popular **Ruby Skye** *(see p110)* – the rewards are worth the wait.

A New Twist

Along with a new breed of "expert mixologists", specialty cocktails are everywhere. Try the **Tonga Room** *(see p107)* and **Martuni's** *(see p113)*, where drinks like Hibiscus-infused vodka and chocolate martinis are gaining in popularity. For a more classic straight-up with a twist, **The Red Room**'s *(see p109)* signature cocktail never fails to charm.

The Beautiful People

While SF is by nature unpretentious, it has its share of fashionable bars. In luxe lounges like **MatrixFillmore** *(see p111)* and **Bambuddha** *(see p109)*, the self-appointed hip elite converge to see and be seen. Hotel bars are especially happening; the Clift's **Redwood Room** *(see p109)* serves a nightly throng of Veuve Clicquot-swilling swells.

choice nightlife

It's Better Live

San Francisco, a catalyst for the explosive counterculture music scene of the 1960s, remains a hotbed of musical innovation. Experimental, indie, and rock acts grace edgy haunts like **Café Du Nord** *(see p112)* and **Club Deluxe** *(see p115)*, while jazz greats play to a dressy, docile crowd at established favorites such as **Harry Denton's** *(see p108)*.

Beer, Beer, and More Beer

Sometimes all you want is a frosty pint and a worn-in bar stool. Luckily, San Francisco and the East Bay have a slew of friendly brew pubs where you can sip all types of amber nectar. **Jupiter** *(see p123)* and the **SF Brewing Co.** *(see p104)* have tempting seasonal selections of beers on tap. And don't miss **Thirsty Bear's** *(see p118)* Valencia Wheat.

Drinking and Dining

You don't have to sacrifice good food for a good drink. The city has plenty of spots that both excite your palate and feed your buzz. Try **Bubble Lounge** *(see p106)* for sophisticated small plates (think caviar, oysters, and foie gras) to go with its champagne and sparkling wines, or **Perry's** *(see p113)*, which has the best tiny burgers ("sliders") in town.

Tosca Café _bohemian opera bar_ `2 E4`

242 Columbus Avenue • 415 391 1244
Open 5pm–2am Tue–Sun

Tosca is a decades-old refuge, known and loved across the city for its old jukebox filled with opera arias on real vinyl platters. A dozen or so red leather booths are arranged across a vast expanse of hardwood floor and the high ceiling makes for an airy space that never seems cramped, even when it's full of patrons. On the long wooden bar, tulip-shaped Irish coffee glasses are lined up already charged with whiskey, sugar, and cream. The bartender only needs to add hot coffee and you've got your warming proof against the fog. For those who want their coffee without the kick, the beautiful old espresso machine (the oldest one in San Francisco) is standing by. The clientele is a real mix – no matter what their other musical tastes are, people of all ages flock to Tosca to drink, converse and conspire, and listen to Luciano or Placido reach the third balcony of the heart.

Tony Nik's _lounge lizard's hangout_ `1 D3`

1534 Stockton Street • 415 693 0990
Open 4pm–2am daily

This dark and cozy lounge feels like the kind of place Sinatra and his famous Rat Pack would have patronized in the 1960s. Expert mixologists serve reasonably priced cocktails to locals on their way home from work, and patrons ease into the leather booths to start or end an evening out in North Beach.

San Francisco Brewing Company `2 E4`

155 Columbus Avenue • 415 434 3344
≫ www.sfbrewing.com Open 11:30am–2am daily

The oldest brew pub in town, this saloon has been operating in one form or another for nearly a century. Fresh, specialty beers are always on tap, and the decor – mahogany woodwork, beveled mirrors, and stained glass – contrasts with an eclectic mix of patrons to create that unique SF western frontier atmosphere.

Vesuvio *Beat Generation pub* `2 E4`

255 Columbus Avenue • 415 362 3370

>> www.vesuvio.com Open 6am–2am daily

In this most bibulous of American cities there are times when you may rise of a morning and wonder at your indulgences of the night before. If you are in or near North Beach and looking for a bit of hair of the dog, drag your sorry self to Vesuvio, any time after cockcrow. The Bohemian Coffee, made with brandy and amaretto, is said to be sovereign for what ails you, and you are most welcome to bring in your bit of pastry from the shop around the corner.

Vesuvio opened in 1948 as a rather unremarkable beer joint in North Beach, the area also home to the emerging literary phenomenon known as the Beat Generation. Jack Kerouac, the chief bard of that movement, happened in one day on his way to visit Henry Miller, author of such ground-breaking works

as *Tropic of Cancer*. Kerouac holed up at the bar and never made it to Miller's house, and Vesuvio has never been the same. It became a favorite hangout for Beat poets and drifters, and today is decorated with memorabilia and art from the Beat movement.

The building juts out from a small corner on Kerouac Alley, snagging passersby and drawing them into an atmosphere of light that would seem to come from candles, golden and warm against the San Francisco fog. People of every conceivable age, sex, orientation, and walk of life find their way here: sailors, cab drivers, financiers, hookers, politicians, tourists, and neighborhood folk. It's always full and the air seethes with interest, poetry, conversation, and argument. The colors blaze but don't distract, the conversation elevates but does not intimidate, and the beer is not too warm or too cold, but just right. It's the best cheap thrills in town.

Bars & Clubs

Bubble Lounge *champagne bar* `2 E4`
714 Montgomery Street • 415 434 4204
➤➤ www.bubblelounge.com Open 5:30pm–12:30am Mon,
5:30pm–1am Tue, 5:30pm–2am Wed–Fri, 6:30pm–2am Sat

This is the city's only dedicated champagne bar, with a dazzling range of champagnes and sparkling wines from all around the world, but it has much more to offer than just bubbly. There is a respectable list of still wines, specialty martinis, and a full bar. A wide range of shellfish, foie gras, caviar, and other decadent treats can be taken at the bar or one of the coffee tables, or even while standing and conversing. At weekends live DJs provide the soundtrack.

Elegant couches and embroidered chairs line the exposed-brick walls of this old place in what used to be the notorious "Barbary Coast" district, and a mostly professional crowd of mixed-age gathers here most nights for civilized revelry. Note: the dress code is strictly enforced and you'll be turned away for wearing sneakers, sandals, tracksuits, or combat trousers.

Irish Bank *get away from it all* `2 E5`
10 Mark Lane • 415 788 7152
➤➤ www.theirishbank.com Open 11:30am–2am daily

Tucked away down a quiet alley, this traditional Irish pub is a refuge from the intensity of the Financial District. The walls are hung with old photographs, memorabilia, and bric-a-brac, and the bar is occupied by regular customers in for a well-priced pint and a chat. A good selection of hearty pub food is also available.

Nightlife Overview
LA has greater numbers, Las Vegas has more neon, but no city in the western US has a greater diversity or better quality of nighttime entertainment than San Francisco. From the sumptuous ballroom of Harry Denton's Starlight Room *(see p108)* to the Castro's gay clubs and the dive bars of Chinatown, SF is the chief party destination in the region.

For the leading-edge club scene with both DJ bars and live music, head for SoMa. The Mission district is synonymous with Latin music and clubs, while North Beach is one long festival, its streets full of music from swing to opera. Head to the outer neighborhoods like Clement Street or Lower Haight for pubs with beer, darts, and poetry. You'll find a bit of everything in the area around Union Square.

Top of the Mark *dancing in the clouds* `1 D5`

InterContinental Mark Hopkins Hotel, 999 California St.
➤➤ topofthemark.citysearch.com • 415 616 6916
Open 5pm–midnight Sun–Thu, 4pm–1am Fri & Sat

At the city's most famous rooftop lounge and dance floor the decor is casually elegant and – as it's the highest bar in town – the views are stunning. A pianist plays in the early evening, then a band plays swing, ballroom, or jazz. Finger foods are available. **Adm**

Li Po Bar *Chinese dive bar* `2 E4`

916 Grant Avenue • 415 982 0072
Open 2pm–2am daily

A true, old-time Chinatown lair. The lurid decor and sagging old floors could be from a movie about Chinese spies or Doctor Fu Manchu. Local bohemians and Chinatown residents have kept this den of cheap beers, cocktails, and high times going for decades. It can get a bit noisy due to the raucous games of dice.

Tonga Room *Polynesian pleasure palace* `1 D5`

Fairmont Hotel, 950 Mason Street • 415 772 5278
➤➤ www.tongaroom.com
Open 5pm–midnight Sun–Thu, 5pm–1am Fri & Sat

This supper club is a favorite with those who want to dress up and not take themselves too seriously. It's a faux South Sea island, with man-made monsoons and a jazz band that wears grass skirts. The best place in town for an umbrella-clad drink served in a coconut.

London Wine Bar *wine and quiet times* `2 F4`

415 Sansome Street • 415 788 4811
➤➤ londonwinebar.citysearch.com Open 11:30am–9pm Mon–Fri

This was the first wine bar in the nation and offers a good number of vintages, mainly from California producers, at a range of prices. In atmosphere, though, this is really more of a "wine pub." The wood paneling, convivial bar, and high-back booths lack only a dart board and there are ales and stout on tap.

Harry Denton's Starlight Room `2 E5`
Sir Francis Drake Hotel, 450 Powell Street • 415 395 8595
>> www.harrydenton.com Open 6pm–2am daily

This rooftop dance club is one of the glittering highlights of the city's nighttime scene. It's run by Harry Denton – known in San Francisco as "Mr. Nightlife" for his many nocturnal enterprises – and the $10–15 cover admits you to the biggest, plushest party in town. The huge room, surrounded on three sides by big picture windows, is dotted with cocktail tables and lined with velvety banquettes. Tuxedo-clad waiters run relays of skillfully mixed cocktails and vintage wines to people who have dressed to the nines in order to party, party, party. You are admonished, however, that there is "no dancing on the bar unless accompanied by Harry."

All manner of people come to the Starlight Room, and have done so throughout its 60-year history.

Twenty-and thirty-something hipsters rub elbows with retired folk, visitors from across the Bay and across the pond, singles, couples, and parties of 10. Even the odd bohemian stuffed uncomfortably into a suit will come here to drink, dance, munch finger foods, and soak up the energy and ebullience of the most carefree place in town.

The music varies from swing to rock to rap and more. The Starlight Orchestra is the most frequent act, playing a range of jazz, pop, and soul. With the dance floor situated along the mirrors of the western wall, it feels like you're dancing in mid-air.

Reservations are highly recommended in order to ensure a table and arriving early or late will help to avoid the shoulder-to-shoulder crush that can often develop between about 9pm and midnight. Bring small bills for tips to the waiters and coat-checkers. **Adm**

The Red Room *as hip as it gets* `3 D1`

827 Sutter Street • 415 346 7666
Open 5pm–2am Mon–Sat, 7pm–2am Sun

Perhaps the city's most popular martini bar, the Red Room is named for its decor, which seems inspired in equal parts by *Playboy* magazine and *Architectural Digest*. A youngish, well-dressed, and very hip crowd often waits in line to be admitted for the giant cocktails and convivial atmosphere. Go early.

Redwood Room *see and be seen* `3 D1`

Clift Hotel, 495 Geary Street • 415 929 2372
>> www.clifthotel.com
Open 5pm–2am Sun–Thu, 4pm–2am Fri & Sat

With its stately redwood-paneled walls and bar this was once the preserve of the brandy and cigar set. Now a young and hip crowd of professionals comes to enjoy an excellent cosmopolitan or martini. It's densely packed most nights so it's best to come early.

Bambuddha Lounge *too hip to quantify* `3 C2`

601 Eddy Street • 415 885 5088
>> www.bambuddhalounge.com
Open 6–11pm Tue–Sat (to 2am Fri & Sat)

Located in the Phoenix Hotel *(see p154)*, Bambuddha Lounge features a superb sound system, well-mixed drinks, and an ample dance floor. It draws a hip crowd who come to party alongside the touring bands who stay in the hotel. **Adm**

Live Music Bars

In North Beach check out **The Saloon** (Map 2 E3, 1232 Grant Ave., 415 989 7666). Established in 1861, it looks disreputable – and that's why you should go there, as well as for the loud blues music for which it is famed. Travelers from all over find their way to the **Gold Dust Lounge** (Map 3 E1, 247 Powell St., 415 397 1695). The music is live every night and people tend to sing along in their native tongues. **Pier 23** (Map 2 F2, at Pier 23 on the Embarcadero, between Green and Battery streets, 415 362 5125, www.pier23cafe.com) is the favorite place for old-time jazz, as well as sharp instrumentals, depending on the night. **Yoshi's** *(see p99)* on the Embarcadero in Oakland has played host to many jazz greats like B.B. King and Pat Metheny.

Ruby Skye *elegant high-tech club*   `3 D1`
420 Mason Street • 415 693 0777
>> www.rubyskye.com Open 7pm–2am Thu–Sat (to 4am Fri & Sat), special events scheduled other nights

Located only a two-minute walk from Union Square, Ruby Skye thrives in an area where there's much competition for the night wanderer's attention. This is a place for people who – in the words of the owner – are "grown-up, make money, and dress nice" to dance the night away, drink fine drinks, smoke a cigar, gossip, and be seen. Originally built as a theater in the 19th century, it still is a very theatrical venue, but brought up-to-date with the latest technology in lighting and sound. The leading-edge decor has built upon the original Victorian influence rather than discarding it, streamlining and coloring to please a more modern eye.

The place is huge, accommodating nearly 1,000 people in all. There are two levels, with four different public rooms complemented by several VIP areas. There is also a separate cognac lounge and – while smoking is banned in most public places in the city – here there is a dedicated cigar bar.

Any evening at Ruby Skye is a special occasion – drinking, dancing, flirting, and boozing are almost art forms here. Just watching the swelling scene in the main room is a thrill – nowhere will you see so many well dressed and drop-dead beautiful people outside of Hollywood. **Adm**

Buena Vista Café *historic watering hole* `1 B2`

2765 Hyde Street • 415 474 5044
>> www.thebuenavista.com
Open 9am–2am Mon–Fri, 8am–2am Sat & Sun

This former saloon wears its patina of age very well. A hardwood floor accommodates a long bar, and a row of chunky wooden tables next to high picture windows gives a great view of the Bay. The Buena Vista is famous for its Irish coffee but also serves lunch and dinner.

Caffe Trieste *cozy refuge in Little Italy* `2 E3`

609 Vallejo Street • 415 982 2605
>> www.caffetrieste.com
Open 6:30am–11pm Sun–Thu, to midnight Fri

Trieste is an irrepressibly convivial neighborhood haunt, where the aroma of espresso seems to be soaked into the walls. Rather small and intimate, it's often crowded with dedicated regulars, especially when local musicians drop by to jam.

MatrixFillmore *singles' rendezvous* `8 H2`

3138 Fillmore Street • 415 563 4180
>> www.plumpjack.com/fill1.html Open 5:30pm–2am nightly

This bar attracts a youngish crowd of affluent people, looking for love or quality time with like-minded peers over fine wine or skillfully mixed cocktails. The fireplace, stonework, and warm woodwork create a stylish environment and the bar menu, served between 5:30 and 11:30pm, is heavy on sushi and other finger foods.

CC's Pierce Street Manor *homey pub* `8 G2`

3243 Pierce Street • 415 346 3523
Open 4pm–2am Mon–Fri, 1pm–2am Fri & Sat

This neighborhood pub is like a return to your childhood home. It is strewn with throw pillows, and full of coffee tables, old lamps, and foot stools. Regulars crowd in here every night to drink draft beers and gin and tonics while playing the imitation antique jukebox. In fine weather the backyard terrace is popular.

Bars & Clubs

Café du Nord   *drinking, DJs, and poetry*   `5 A1`
2170 Market Street • 415 861 5016
>> www.cafedunord.com
Open 1 hour before showtime to 2am nightly

There are certain places that have their finger to the wind and simply know what's coming down the culture and style pike. Café du Nord has been doing that since the 1920s when it was a speakeasy, serving bathtub gin to jazz babies as they danced the Charleston. It was a leader of the swing revival in the 1990s, and today is at the cutting edge of live dance music, as well as spoken word performance, and caters to mainly Gen-X and Gothic crowds.

  In this basement cabaret, oil paintings are illuminated by converted gas lamps and lovers snuggle on antique couches as they call for well-made cocktails, though there are also plenty of well-dressed singles here. The dinner served is nothing remarkable, but it's certainly not bad. It's the ambience that makes a visit worthwhile. **Adm**

Jade   *Asian-chic cocktail lounge*   `3 B3`
650 Gough Street • 415 869 1900
>> www.jadebar.com   Open 5pm–2am Mon–Sat, 8pm–2am Sun

The colors and hues in this over-the-top Asian-themed fantasy lair perfectly call to mind that green gemstone. One look at the elegant and well-dressed young Hayes Valley crowd brings to mind dollar green as well, as they sip creative cocktails, munch "Asian tapas," and chat by the interior koi carp pool.

Mad Dog in the Fog   *popular British pub*   `10 H2`
530 Haight Street • 415 626 7279
Open 11:30am–2am Mon–Fri, 10am–2am Sat & Sun

This pub with a huge beer selection is an anchor of the Lower Haight, and on some nights it seems home away from home for many expat Londoners. Arguments about literature spring up as often as those about sports, DJs spin on Friday nights, and the place even manages to draw a crowd on Sunday nights.

For the very latest on San Francisco go to >> www.realcity.dk.com

Orbit Room *airy cocktail bar* `3 B5`
1900 Market Street • 415 252 9525
Open 8am–2am Mon–Sat, 9am–2am Sun

Bohemian San Francisco meets the cocktail set in this rotunda-like bar with its Art Deco flourishes and fine paintings hung from the great circular wall. Bicycle messengers, web designers, budding filmmakers, and the odd hooker convene here for classic cocktails and perhaps a *panino* before the kitchen closes at 10pm.

Perry's *traditional bar and grill* `8 H2`
1944 Union Street • 415 922 9022
>> www.perrysunionst.citysearch.com Open from 9am daily

This old-time place offering good pub grub and beer is more than just a pick-up joint. Brasswork, old woodwork, and checkered tablecloths make it a homey place for a drink and a bite to eat, and the dark mahogany bar is a great place for friends to meet, to commence or close an evening out in the Marina.

Martuni's *metrosexual piano bar* `5 B1`
4 Valencia Street • 415 241 0205
>> www.martunis.citysearch.com Open 4pm–2am daily

On the cusp of the Castro and Mission districts, Martuni's straddles the two contrasting worlds of the blue-collar immigrant community and the sensual and art-filled life of gay San Francisco. This is a place that welcomes all kinds of people to its deep, dark, musical heart. Here is the casual elegance that San Francisco is so well known for. The crowd, roughly half gay and half straight, is an eclectic mix of people from all quarters: artists, writers, bankers, neighborhood folk, even the occasional tourist, though it's off the beaten path for nightlife and so is generally known only to locals. Men don jackets and ladies their killer skirts to enter the black-lit sanctum of the piano bar, where a martini is the size of a cornucopia and where the pianist is ready to play almost any song you may wish to hear – or sing. It's what karaoke wishes it were.

Bars & Clubs

The Café *buzzing bar liked by gay girls* `10 H3`
2367 Market Street • 415 861 3846
>> www.clubesf.com Open 4pm–2am daily (from 3pm Sat & Sun)

Upstairs and overlooking the Castro, SF's famous gay neighborhood, this place once catered mainly to gay women. Now it is mixed and all are welcome to dance in the dark or shoot a game of pool. Drinks are easy on the wallet and patrons easy on the eyes. It's a high energy place, so don't come for relaxation.

Harvey's *San Francisco's original gay bar* `10 H4`
500 Castro Street • 415 431 4278
Open 11am–2am Mon–Fri, 9am–2am Sat & Sun

Perhaps the most famous gay bar in San Francisco, this was named for the late Harvey Milk, the first openly gay politician in the city. A neighborhood pub, serving decent pub grub during the day, it's a good place for a pint and a snack. Political posters and other memorabilia offer a bit of local history with the beer.

GLBT San Francisco

Utter the name of San Francisco and three people out of 10 will first think "gay bar!" And that's not entirely without cause. The city of Saint Francis has since its beginning embraced people who were out of the mainstream. For decades now the city has welcomed, and protected, all manner of persons whose sexual orientation is other than traditional.

Long ago places catering to gay men were concentrated mainly in the Castro district. Nowadays, no matter where you are, nobody bats an eye at gay couples or groups out on the town. And so many married-with-children straight people have moved into the Castro that some gay folk grouse about it.

No place is entirely gay or straight anymore – indeed the city's most famous gay bar, **Harvey's** *(see above)*, looks like any neighborhood pub. Still, there are places that cater to an almost exclusively gay clientele. **The Stud** (Map 3 D4, 399 9th St.,

www.studsf.com) is perhaps the gayest of gay nightspots in town. Hard male bodies in varying states of undress gyrate on the dance floor to equally hard rock and rap. The air is redolent of sweat, hormones, and beer. "Gendernauts" entertain at the weekly "tranny-shack" drag party, and the odd straight couple makes out at the bar.

The Bar on Castro (Map 10 H3, 456 Castro St.) thunders with sound for a surprisingly small dance floor – it's usually full of happy horny people. Red Bull energy drink is the aphrodisiac of choice here, backed up by designer vodka. At **Kimo's** (Map 3 B1, 1351 Polk St.) the once-popular drag shows have been replaced by live punk, indie and alt-rock music. The tiny **Phone Booth** (Map 5 C5, 1398 South Van Ness Ave.) in the Mission is a favorite hangout for both girls looking for girls and boys looking for boys. The drink of choice here is Anchor Steam beer and music includes the likes of Nirvana.

Zam Zam *cocktail culture in beerland* `10 F2`
1633 Haight Street • 415 861 2545
Open 3pm–2am Mon–Fri, 1pm–2am Sat & Sun

This elegant, Persian-inspired cocktail lounge, with its plush booths and heavy draperies, is an anomaly in the Haight-Ashbury district. Outside may be blue-collar and psychedelic, but in here it's all arched portals, mirrors, and gold tassel trim. The ghosts of the Grateful Dead may haunt the street, but in here Sinatra still croons on the juke box.

The original proprietor, Bruno Mooshei, was a legendary San Francisco character, who kept the bar just as it was when it opened in 1941 and was famous for refusing service to those he didn't like the look of. The new owners, while retaining the 40s aesthetic, are rather more accommodating. Men and women of all backgrounds and ages dress the part and come from across town to sip well-priced martinis, cosmopolitans, and margaritas in Zam Zam's luxurious recesses or at the large horseshoe bar.

Club Deluxe *swing club in hippieville* `10 F2`
1511 Haight Street • 415 552 6949
» www.clubdeluxesf.com
Open 6pm–2am Mon–Fri, 2pm–2am Sat & Sun

A visit to this small but classy venue is like stepping back into the 1940s. Cocktails are served at the bar and in the adjacent lounge area you can swing dance with zoot-suited hipsters to the music of Glenn Miller and Count Basie, played anew by local bands.

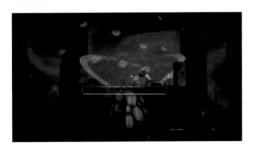

Mezzanine *hipster dance & art destination* `4 E2`
444 Jessie Street • 415 625 8880
» www.mezzaninesf.com Hours vary depending on performances; check website for schedules

This huge club boasts the leading edge in sound, lighting, and laser technologies, and showcases music from all genres. Even DJs vie with each other to get into the place. Acres of wall space exhibit a continuing rotation of art, film, and multimedia shows.

Bars & Clubs

The EndUp · *all-welcoming after-hours club* · `4 E3`
401 6th Street • 415 646 0999
» www.theendup.com Open 9pm–4am Wed, 10pm–4:30am
Thu, 10pm–6am Fri, 9pm–6am Sat, 6am–4am Sun

A late night hot spot that defies pigeon-holing, EndUp is
the favorite after-party party of the city's most dedicated
club hoppers. The small dance floor often spills out
onto the terrace, which is also a popular lounge spot on
warm days. Dress in anything from leather to black tie.

Buzz 9 · *relaxed neighborhood lounge* · `3 D4`
139 8th Street • 415 255 8783
» www.buzz9.com Open 6pm–1:30am Tue–Sat

This is a roomy, underground bar where a very mixed
crowd likes to mingle over martinis and beer. The easy
chairs and sofas are popular with local literati and up-
and-coming artists who tend to use it as a communal
living room. It is underneath a restaurant of the same
name which serves Californian cuisine and cocktails.

Thirsty Bear · *artisan beer and world music* · `4 F2`
661 Howard Street • 415 974 0905
» www.thirstybear.com Open 11:30am–10pm Mon–Thu,
11:30am–midnight Fri, noon–midnight Sat, 5pm–10pm Sun

Industrial chic is alive and well in the city of Saint
Francis, especially in this high-energy brew pub.
Music, conversation, and general hubbub bounce off
the brick walls and the stainless steel brewing tanks
as waiters thread their way through thick crowds to
deliver tasty Spanish tidbits to the mixed bunch that
packs the Thirsty Bear every night.

   All the world knows that California is a major wine
producer, but it's also an important brewing center, with
San Francisco leading the lot. While there is a full bar
here, and an extensive wine list, it's the beer that the
T-Bear is famous for. Among the house brews IPA is
one of the constants, while many change seasonally.
The brewmaster is always experimenting: "We just
think beer," he says. The background music changes,
too, ranging from klezmer to jazz to flamenco.

Duplex *stylish SoMa spot* `3 C4`
1525 Mission Street • 415 615 6888
≫ www.duplexsf.com
Open 9pm–3am Tue–Thu, 9pm–4am Fri & Sat

Decorated in moody tones, this progressive club mixes traditional and modern touches like vintage mirrors and computer graphic projections. Jet-setters (and wannabes) dance to international DJ sets: everything from funk and Latin house to the latest hip-hop. **Adm**

12 Galaxies *live music bar* `5 C4`
2565 Mission Street • 415 970 9777
≫ www.12galaxies.com
Open 4pm–2am Mon–Fri, 11am–2am Sat & Sun

Popular with music aficionados, 12 Galaxies attracts up-and-coming local and national indie acts. DJs spin too, and the intimate performance space is ringed by small tables. The bar area is more open, but you can cozy up and chill out on the balcony upstairs. **Adm**

Make-Out Room *music, pool, no stress* `5 C4`
3225 22nd Street • 415 647 2888
≫ www.makeoutroom.com Open 6pm–2am daily

Make-Out is a neo-bohemian hipster bar. It's easy on the wallet and makes for a popular place to wind down after an evening of intensity. The cavernous room is scattered with furnishings and populated by dressed-down people, and there are regular performances by local musicians of every genre.

Metronome Dance Center *ballroom* `6 F2`
1830 17th Street • 415 252 9000
≫ www.metronomedancecenter.com Open 10:30am–9pm
Mon–Fri, 10am–11pm Sat, 10am–6pm Sun

This huge studio space houses the two largest dance floors in the city. During the day on weekends and every weeknight, classes are held in all the classics – waltz, tango, swing, and foxtrot – and on Fridays there's an evening ball. Soft drinks only. **Adm**

Bars & Clubs

Bottom of the Hill *music & dance venue* `6 G1`
1233 17th Street • 415 621 4455
>> www.bottomofthehill.com Open from 4pm Wed–Fri, from 8:30pm Sat–Tue (happy hour 4–7pm Wed–Fri)

A modest cover charge gets you into what is arguably the best place for live music, of all genres, in San Francisco. You can drink, shoot pool, dance, and have a bite for just a few dollars. The atmosphere is intimate and the crowd is always unpretentious. **Adm**

Elbo Room *classic pub with live music* `5 B2`
647 Valencia Street • 415 552 7788
>> www.elbo.com Open 5pm–2am nightly

Downstairs is a neighborhood pub always thick with conviviality, beer drinking, and pool shooting. But upstairs it's a bohemian dance club with some of the best dancers, and musicians, in the Bay Area. Live bands and DJs play every night. The music is heavy on Latin, though many other genres play as well.

Cocktails and Culture

Nobody really knows how or where it started, but there are many places in this city where people come to enjoy both high art and a drink. In San Francisco you just can't separate fine art and the art of the party, and it often seems that a martini glass is an indispensible accessory. No one raises an eyebrow at the mixing of cocktails and a bit of dancing amid exhibitions of sculpture, painting and other arts.

Rx Gallery (Map 3 D2, 132 Eddy St., 415 474 7973, www.rxgallery.com) is both a bar serving beer, wine, and sake, and a gallery that features not only exhibitions but the odd musical performance by solo artists or duets, usually acoustic. The bar opens at 5pm, Wed–Sat.

Hotel Biron (Map 3 B4, 45 Rose St., 415 703 0403, www.hotelbiron.com), little more than a hole in the wall, is part bistro, part museum. A new artist is featured each month, and the wine list is extensive. You can have a bit of caviar or cheese, and a glass of bubbly or still wine, as you consider a purchase of fine art or just sit back and admire it.

The Canvas Gallery and Café (Map 9 D3, 1200 9th Ave., 415 504 0060, www.thecanvasgallery. com) has jumped on the sake bandwagon of late, but it is also a wine lounge with leading-edge art for admiration and for sale. It's a total art venue, with painting, sculpture, music, spoken word, comedy, and other forms of entertainment on offer, along with the drinks. The café has a selection of salads, sandwiches, and pasta dishes.

When you're tired of high art, try **Fly Bar** (Map 10 G1, 762 Divisadero St., 415 931 4359). Beer, sake, cocktails, sangria, pizza, and pasta are served amid jazzy paintings and murals of people in the world of music. This place is also open during the day, so it is good for lunch or a snack, or a cold beer on a summer afternoon, as well as an art fix.

Wild Side West *lesbian bar welcoming all*
242 Cortland Avenue • 415 647 3099 • MUNI 24 from Divisadero
Open 1pm–2am daily

This charming saloon on Potrero Hill is chiefly a
neighborhood lesbian haunt, but everyone who
doesn't care about their own sexuality or anyone
else's is also more than welcome. People of all ages,
styles, walks of life, and sexual preference come here
to enjoy the well-priced cocktails and beer.

Being off the usual tourist path, few out-of-towners
manage to find their way to Wild Side West, though
many hear about it. The old-style decor is homey,
with a polished wooden bar, globe lamps, and
panelled walls, but appropriately cutthroat
competitions take place around the bright-red pool
table. In the wintertime it's the coziest of cozy, with
comfy furniture and not too much noise. The garden
patio in the back offers numerous little nooks and
crannies for snuggling and stealing kisses, even in
not-so-fine weather. No credit cards, cash only.

Zeitgeist *chilled-out biker bar*   `3 B5`
199 Valencia Street • 415 255 7505
>> zeitgeist.citysearch.com Open 9am–2am daily

Market Street is busy by day and so is Valencia. But
when night descends there are few islands of light in
this gritty area but for Martuni's *(see p113)* and the
venerable Zeitgeist. Basically a pub, this is the unofficial
headquarters of the city's bicycle messengers and a
hang-out for students and artsy types on the rise,
although people of all stripes are made welcome.

There are some 30 different beers on tap, many
from local microbreweries like Anderson Valley and
Coast Range, and the walls are festooned with
posters and signs ("Boobs, not bombs"). Indeed the
bartenders themselves are adorned with much
artwork in the form of tattoos.

In fine weather those not watching TV or shooting
pool can migrate to the eucalyptus-shaded beer
garden at the rear where there are rows of outdoor
seating and a BBQ serving great grill food.

Bars & Clubs

El Rio *ultra-cool drink and dance joint* `5 C5`
3158 Mission Street • 415 282 3325
>> www.elriosf.com
Open 4 or 5pm–2am Mon–Fri, by event Sat, 3pm–2am Sun

Ironically billing itself as "your dive," El Rio is anything but a dive. The thrift store-clad and the well-attired equally await the bouncer's blessing to enter this multi-ethnic, multi-sexual dance and drinking venue. Prices are small; so are the drinks.

The Plough and Stars *real Irish pub* `7 D5`
116 Clement Street • 415 751 1122
>> www.theploughandstars.com
Open 4pm–2am Mon, 2pm–2am Tue–Thu, noon–2am Fri–Sun

Step through these doors and into Ireland. You'll hear the brogue coming from all corners, especially on the nights when Irish poets perform their own works and those of the ancients. The stout flows, the darts fly, and now and then the whole company breaks into song.

Trad'r Sam's *kitsch elevated to art* `7 A5`
6150 Geary Boulevard • 415 221 0773
Open 11am–2am daily

Out westward on outer Geary Boulevard, beyond the glamour and glitz of downtown, and with "respectable" San Francisco far behind it, lies an institution that used to be just one of many of its wild and crazy kind. Trad'r Sam's is now almost the last of the "Tiki Bars," those Polynesian-themed hideaways, replete with potted palms, carved wooden idols, burning torches on the back patio, and rum cocktails with names like Scorpion, Planter's Punch, and Mai Tai.

Established in 1939, Trad'r Sam's is considered a cultural icon now, and well-dressed hipsters wait in line to enter this alcoholic anachronism and ensconce themselves in the battered beach chairs and hideaway booths. The bar is bathed in red light, spotted with idols and palm fronds, and hung with tropical flowers (faux though they be). The crowd is boozy but not too boisterous.

For the very latest on San Francisco go to >> www.realcity.dk.com

Jupiter *musical microbrew pub*
2181 Shattuck Avenue, Berkeley • 510 843 8277
BART to Downtown Berkeley
>> www.jupiterbeer.com Open 11:30am–1am Mon–Fri
(to 1:30am Fri), noon–1:30am Sat, 1pm–midnight Sun

The interior of this brick building is furnished with old
church pews. Some two dozen microbrews accompany
the comfort foods from the wood-burning oven, and
the live music ranges from bluegrass to fusion jazz.

The Alley *venerable piano dive*
3325 Grand Ave., Oakland • 510 444 8505 • No. 58 AC Transit Bus
Open 11am–2am daily

Step into The Alley and you'll find that it's aptly named.
This really is a bit of a dive – cavernous, dark, and
shabby – though no one would change it. Pianist Rod
Dibble has been fingering the keys here for decades
and he can play anything you might want to sing along
to. A cheap dinner menu is available in the evenings.

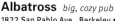

Albatross *big, cozy pub*
1822 San Pablo Ave., Berkeley • 510 843 2473 • BART to
Downtown Berkeley, then No. 9 AC Transit Bus
>> www.albatrosspub.com
Open 6pm–2am Sun–Tue, 4:30pm–2am Wed–Sat

Berkeley's oldest pub welcomes poor students and
well-heeled visitors alike. It has the air of a large,
rambling country house and offers board games, a
darts league, microbrews, and a place to feel at home.

Kingman's Lucky Lounge *neighborhood bar*
3332 Grand Ave., Oakland • 510 465 5464 • No. 58 AC Transit Bus
Open 5pm–2am nightly

Dark and narrow, its walls lined with couches and
easy chairs, this is the neighborhood's living room
with bar service. DJs spin every night after 8:30pm,
playing a wide variety of house, jazz, hip-hop, and
other styles. The atmosphere is very relaxed and the
diverse crowd likes to dress up just a bit.

Heinold's First and Last Chance Saloon *historic watering hole*
56 Jack London Square, Oakland • 510 839 6761 • BART to
12th St., then 10 minute walk west Open noon–midnight daily

A small place on the waterfront where writer Jack
London used to raise hell in his outlaw days. The 1906
earthquake caused the south end of the floor to sink
3 ft (1 m), so watch that first step. Leave all pretensions
at the door, order a simple drink, and enjoy.

>> *A short distance from Heinold's on Jack London Square is Yoshi's jazz club (see p99)*

streetlife

Life happens out on the streets in San Francisco. All of the city's districts have their own distinct appeal, from the colorful markets of Chinatown, to the genteel worlds of Russian Hill and Noe Valley, and the bright lights of North Beach at night. The city's compact layout means it's easy to navigate on foot, but if you tire of the hills you can always jump on to one of the famous cable cars.

Streetlife

North Beach *Little Italy* 1 D3

North Beach was settled by Italians who make an art of living well, and locals and visitors alike come here to have a good time, day and night.

The whole of the neighborhood exudes the spirit of Italy, but each of its main streets has a distinct character. Broadway is the best known street. It's where the city's high-end strip clubs are located, bold with neon. The most famous of these was the Condor which is now home to **Andrew Jaeger's House of Seafood and Jazz** (entry at 300 Columbus Ave., www. condorsf.com). But it's not all sex and the city on Broadway. **Black Oak Books** (540 Broadway, www. blackoakbooks.com) sells a wealth of new and used books, and where Broadway reaches Powell, the **Imperial Tea Court** (1411 Powell St., *see p138*) is a great place for a quiet hour in the afternoon. In the evening when the fog rolls in people head for **Enrico's** (504 Broadway, www.enricossidewalkcafe.com) for Irish coffee under heat lamps on the sidewalk and Italian

fare inside. Grant Avenue lies immediately around the corner from Broadway and yet seems like another town. It's darker, quieter, and less Italian than other streets. Day-trippers come here to shop: **Old Vogue** (No. 1412) carries superior vintage clothing, while next door **101 Music** (No. 1414) offers music for collectors on cassette and vinyl, including 45s. **AB Fits** (No. 1519, *see p53*) is the place for denim, while across the street **Asia Galleries** (No. 1534, asiagalleries.com) houses a fine selection of Asian antiques. The old-time **Italian French Bakery** (No. 1501) is there for those who need an afternoon bite, and for coffee or a glass of wine nothing beats **Caffe Trieste** (609 Vallejo St., *see p111*). Old saloons, such as the aptly named **The Saloon** (No. 1232), and a few cozy singles clubs like **Savoy Tivoli** (No. 1434) attract night wanderers to this shadowy lane.

Columbus Avenue runs diagonally right through the heart of Little Italy, and if it weren't for the fog it would feel like any street in Italy. It's lined with

restaurants and cafés, most with sidewalk seating beneath heat lamps. The northern half of the avenue is tree-lined and deeply shaded, sheltering small trattorias such as **L'Osteria del Forno** (No. 519). Nearby, **Mara's Italian Pastry** (No. 503) is great for a snack during a walkabout. Locals favor **Mario's Bohemian Cigar Store** (No. 566) for lunch or afternoon coffee. Buskers sing and play here more than any other part of the city, and range from strolling mariachi bands to ex-cons singing gospel. Near the southern end a collection of bars and small clubs keeps the evening lively: **Tosca Café** (No. 242, *see p104*) has a unique jukebox full of opera hits, and **Spec's** bar (12 William Saroyan Place) adds to the buzz. **Jazz at Pearl's** (256 Columbus Ave., *see p88*) combines live soft jazz and a Spanish-inspired tapas menu in an elegant atmosphere.

Stockton Street brings you to Washington Square, which is dominated by the Italianesque façade of the **Saints Peter and Paul Church**. The square is a fine bit of open space, where practioners of tai chi go through their morning exercises. The aroma of focaccia from **Liguria Bakery** (1700 Stockton St.) seems to blanket the whole square, and office workers often bring their lunches to the green. Some of the city's best eateries are on the square, including **Moose's** (No. 1652, www.mooses.com) and **Washington Square Bar & Grill** (1707 Powell St., www.wsbg.citysearch.com).

To the north of North Beach lies **Fisherman's Wharf** (Map 1 C2). While some fishing boats still land their catches here, the area is mainly a tourist attraction. However it's still a photogenic place to come for lunch with a view – try the **Eagle Café** (Pier 39, www.pier39.com.) The **Musée Mécanique** (Pier 45, www.musee mechanique.org) – a collection of antique arcade and carnival attractions – and the excellent **Aquarium of the Bay** (Pier 39, www.aquariumofthe bay.com) are both worth a visit. A colony of sea lions has taken over part of Pier 39 – even some locals will admit to having come to watch them at least once.

Streetlife

Chinatown *mercantile merriment* 2 E4

This swathe of territory from the Chinatown Gateway on Bush Street to the cusp of Little Italy *(see pp126–7)* at Broadway is home to the second-largest Chinese community in the western hemisphere. It's densely packed and virtually undrivable, but perfect for navigating on foot. Grant Avenue, considered the main drag, is jammed with shops carrying all kinds of Chinese merchandise, knick-knacks, and the kind of junk you'll want to rid yourself of when you get home. One place not to miss however is the **Chinatown Kite Shop** (No. 717, www.chinatownkite.com). Here you'll find flying bits of whimsy in an astonishing array of shapes and colors – perfect for taking out to the Marina Green *(see p140)* on a blustery day.

One block west of Grant is Stockton Street, where the Chinese come to shop. It's a scene of organized chaos as vegetable and fish markets, restaurants, herbalists, and shops purveying all things required by a Chinese household spill out on to the street. Frenetic shopping can work up an appetite so have a snack at **Louie's Dim Sum** (No. 1242), or for a more substantial lunch try Yuet Lee Seafood (No. 1300).

The **Chinese Historical Society of America** (www.chsa.org) has a museum at 965 Clay Street exploring the role of the Chinese community in the US. But the best place to get a true sense of Chinatown itself is in the shadowy "Chinatown alleyways" between Grant and Stockton, where makers of fortune cookies and concocters of herbal potions sell their wares. Drop into the **Tin How Temple** *(see p70)*, have a dress made to order at **Hong Chin Dress Makers** (810 Clay St.), or shop for exotic musical instruments at **Clarion Music Center** (816 Sacramento St., www.clarionmusic.com). In the evening a Chinese feast awaits at **Far East Café** (631 Grant Ave., www.fareastcafesf.com).

Russian Hill *charming residential district* `1 C3`

This is an area of steep and twisting streets, beautiful buildings with row upon row of bay windows, and a host of small galleries and hidden-away parks. The section of **Lombard Street** near the summit of Russian Hill (pictured right), known as "the crookedest street in the world," zigzags up an incline of 40 degrees. Round the corner, the **Diego Rivera Gallery** in the SF Art Institute (800 Chestnut St., www.sfai.edu) houses works by the famed muralist, while further south **Ina Coolbrith Park** (Map 1 D3) has little paths and beautiful gardens.

This is a great area to wander around admiring the gorgeous houses and some of the city's most stunning views of **Coit Tower** *(see p73)* and **Alcatraz Island** *(see p12)*. The original **Swenson's** ice creamery at 1999 Hyde Street is the place to stop if you're in need of refreshment. Hyde Street is the commerical hub of the area, and here you'll also find restaurants like **Zarzuela** (No. 2000), the queen of the city's Spanish restaurants, and **Sushi Groove** (No. 1916), a hip Japanese joint.

Clement Street *the new Chinatown* `7 D5`

The stretch of Clement Street between Arguello and Park Presidio has gone through a renaissance in recent years. This once predominantly Italian and Irish neighborhood is now home to Asian groceries and restaurants which sit alongside the pubs and coffee houses. They don't replace the area's old world character, but add to it, producing a rich "Eurasian" mix.

The fresh seafood and condiments found in the Asian groceries are a draw, but shoppers also come here for the superb collection of rare books at **Green Apple Books** (No. 506, *see p61*). Another reason to visit is the restaurants, which offer a wide range of cuisines. **Burma Superstar** (No. 309, www.burma superstar.com) is one of the brightest lights, with spicy, colorful fare at most reasonable prices, while people from all over the city come to the upscale **Clementine** (No. 126) for a taste and feel of France. Most of Clement closes rather early, but **The Plough and Stars** pub (No. 116, *see p122*) draws beer until the wee hours.

>> *See www.sanfranciscochinatown.com for information about events in Chinatown*

Streetlife

Marina *high-end shops and buzzing bars* `8 G1`

There is an actual marina here where people dock their boats, but when locals talk about "the Marina" they mean the rectangle on the map bounded by Union, Baker, and Laguna streets and Marina Boulevard. On weekends Frisbees fly on **Marina Green** *(see p140)*, and pick-up volleyball goes on through the day at nearby **Crissy Field** *(see p142)*. Chestnut Street is the area's main shopping strip, where the chief trade is in informal but pricy apparel and high-end homewares. You'll also find **Little Tibet** (No. 2385), popular for imported Asian goods, **The Humidor** (No. 2050), one of the remaining high-end tobacconists in town, and **Books Inc.** (No. 2251, www.booksinc.net), a favorite local haunt. Off Chestnut, **Plump Jack Wines** (3201 Fillmore St., www.plumpjack.com) carries a wide selection of wines from around the world.

Chestnut Street has many handsome buildings; relatively new structures which were put up after the 1906 earthquake. Many are admirable examples of Art Deco architecture. The district is also home to some architectural oddities, such as the eight-sided **Octagon House** (2645 Gough St.), built in 1861, and the **Vedanta Hindu Temple** (Map 8 H1, 2963 Webster St.) of 1905. The **Palace of Fine Arts** *(see p73)* on the edge of the Presidio was designed by architect Bernard Maybeck in 1915 to represent a classical ruin.

At night the Marina is mainly known for its singles' scene, and there are plenty of bars around Union Street catering to a well-funded heterosexual crowd. **Perry's** (No. 1944, *see p113*) is one of the oldest, while the latest and greatest, **MatrixFillmore** (3138 Fillmore St., *see p111*), is around the corner. For a nighttime bite, best bets are **Izzy's Steak and Chop House** (3345 Steiner St., www.izzyssteaksandchops.com), an institution jammed with locals nightly, and **Mel's Drive-In** (2165 Lombard St., www.melsdrive-in.com), a quintessential burger joint.

For the very latest on San Francisco go to ≫ **www.realcity.dk.com**

Lower Haight *defiantly un-hip* `10 H2`

Lower Haight lies at the eastern end of the Haight-Ashbury district, which was famously the home of hippies and bohemians in the 1960s. While the Upper Haight basks in its notoriety and Summer of Love past, the Lower Haight relaxes in self-satisfied anonymity. Although it's a bit gritty and grotty, it is far more interesting and an undiscovered land to visitors.

People are drawn here by the pub grub and beer, flea-market antiques and old vinyl records, folk music and leading-edge DJs. **Mickey's Monkey** (214 Pierce St.) carries "Stuff for Your Place," as the sign over the door announces. It's an old curiosity shop, stocked by gleaners who follow estate sales and prowl thrift shops. Nearby **Rooky's Records** (448 Haight St., www.rookyricardosrecords.com) is the best place in the city to shop for old 45 rpm vinyl records. The range is huge, and spans decades of pop music. Comic book fans will find the classics at **Comix Experience** (305 Divisadero, www.comixexperience.com). **Mad Dog in the Fog** (530 Haight St., *see p112*) is the people's pub, with live music and a great range of beers, while the **Noc Noc** "cave bar" (557 Haight St.) and **Underground SF** (424 Haight St. www.undergroundsf.com) are two of the many DJ-bars in the area.

Dining in the Lower Haight is more like dining in somebody's home than going out to eat, and the area is known for its international cuisines. **Kate's Kitchen** (471 Haight St.) is a favorite for a huge breakfast at a small price. **Axum Café** (698 Haight St., www.axum cafe.com) offers Ethiopian fare, with storefront windows that look out on to the passing scene. **Squat & Gobble Café** (237 Fillmore St., www.squatandgobble.com) is great for crepes, while **Thep Phanom** (400 Waller St., www.thepphanom.com) is the neighborhood Thai place.

Streetlife

The Castro *SF's original gay neighborhood* `10 H3`

Only about two blocks of the famous Castro district are actually on Castro Street. Most of it is on Market Street between 17th and Valencia streets, with the very heart of the gay district lying at the confluence of Castro and Market. There are a number of eating and drinking venues here, including **The Café** (2367 Market St., *see p114*), a club popular with gay women, though all are welcome. The view from the upper floors is always good and catches the distinctive hubbub of this high energy district. On Saturday nights the sidewalks are full of residents and visitors who come for the unique party atmosphere. Just don't gawk – some people here dress very unconventionally.

The most celebrated establishment of any kind here is **Harvey's** (500 Castro St., *see p114*), the pub named after the late Harvey Milk, San Francisco's first openly gay elected city official. Some first-time visitors are disappointed to find that it looks like any other pub, with a diverse clientele. The **Badlands** (4121 18th St., www.sfbadlands.com) is more in keeping with most people's idea of a gay bar.

The **Castro Theatre** (429 Castro St., *see p96*) is a real gem in the area. This gorgeous movie palace is a venue for first-release and independent films, as well as an important local society hub. For dinner or lunch **Catch** (2362 Market St., www.catchsf.com) serves the best seafood in the neighborhood, in a cozy, hearth-warmed space. Restaurant **Mecca** (2029 Market St., *see p39*) offers a superb dinner, a circular bar, and occasional cabaret or burlesque entertainment. If shopping is your entertainment **Worn Out West** (582 Castro St.) has a full range of cowboy wear, police wear, leather jackets, and fatigues.

Noe Valley *small town in the big city*   `5 A5`

A self-contained "village" bisected by 24th and Church streets, and seemingly cut off from the rest the of city by steep hills on all sides, Noe Valley has a delicious feeling of isolation. Postwar construction-boom houses shoulder up to old Victorians, while chi-chi cafés, restaurants, boutiques, and gourmet groceries dot the landscape, making the area a delight to wander around. **Gallery of Jewels** (4089 24th St., www.galleryofjewels. com) specializes in chiefly metallic jewelry: gold, silver, and platinum beaten and rolled into unique shapes. **Chocolate Covered** (3977 24th St.) offers everything chocolate from around the world, while **Stonehouse** (3901 24th St., www.stonehouseoliveoil.com) carries California-grown olives and oil, as well as condiments and utensils. **Global Exchange** (4018 24th St., www. globalexchange.org) deals in environmentally friendly and fair-trade arts and crafts. For lunch try crepes at **Savor** (3913 24th St.) or relax in the garden of **Le Zinc French Bistro** (4063 24th St., www.lezinc.com).

Potrero Hill *neighborhood that's above it all*   `6 F3`

This is a quiet, sunny middle-class neighborhood on the outskirts of the Mission (*see p134*). It has a compact but lively commercial district and many fine old houses. Couple that with great views over the city and this is a fine getaway from the beaten path.

There are several galleries in the area. The **Vista Point Gallery** (405 Florida St., www.vistapointgallery. com) houses a collection of landscape photography, while **Southern Exposure** (401 Alabama St., www. soex.org) is an adventurous non-profit artists' organization. Across the street is the famous **Project Artaud Theater** (450 Florida St., www.artaud.org), a cutting-edge live performance venue.

The nightlife scene here is small and intimate and everybody seems to know each other. A dining star in the emerging firmament is **Aperto** (1434 18th St., www. apertosf.com) with its Italian standards and homey setting. Head to the **Bottom of the Hill** (1233 17th St., *see p120*) for a great live music and dance venue.

>> *Pick up organic food at Noe Valley Farmers' Market (Map 5 A4, 24th St., www.noevalleyfarmersmarket.com)*

Streetlife

The Mission *original San Francisco* `5 C2`

Bounded by Dolores, 16th, South Van Ness, and Cesar Chavez streets, this is where San Francisco began as a Spanish mission settlement. After the American acquisition of California it became a predominately Irish neighborhood and remained so till the 1960s, when Latin American immigrants began to revert it to something more Hispanic. In recent years it has taken on an Asian flavor as well. The result is a very mixed neighborhood, and everybody likes it that way. There's intensive shopping during the day, much of it carried on out on the street (especially along the 2700 block of Mission St.), and a graceful yet unpretentious restaurant and club scene at night.

The old church of **Mission Dolores** (3321 16th St., *see p75*) is San Francisco's oldest building and the embodiment of the city's Spanish colonial roots. Its graveyard, the last resting place of many prominent San Franciscans, was immortalized in Hitchcock's *Vertigo*.

Inside, the church has painted ceilings, a gilded altar, and a small museum displaying historical documents.

The Mission District is also famous for its murals, which reflect the Latino influence on the area. To see the best examples wander along **Balmy Alley** between Folsom, Harrison, 24th, and 25th streets. On 18th Street the **Women's Building** (No. 3543, www.womens building.org) has one of the most impressive facades.

At night walk down Mission, Valencia, 16th, or 24th streets to soak up the spice and music of this artistic and hedonistic hotbed. For a light meal stop at French creperie **Ti Couz** (3108 16th St., *see p42*) or **El Nuevo Fruitlandia** (3077 24th St.), which offers Puerto Rican specialties such as roast pork with yucca. Or go a bit upscale at **Luna Park** (694 Valencia St., *see p42*) where a variety of international comfort foods await. Close the evening with late night live jazz at **Bruno's** (2389 Mission St., www.brunoslive.com) or at **Martuni's** (4 Valencia St., *see p113*), a fun piano bar.

Telegraph Avenue *counterculture*
From the foot of Bancroft Way to Parker Street, Berkeley;
BART to Downtown Berkeley, then 10-minute walk north

Running from the edge of the University of California campus, Telegraph Avenue is where it all happened in the turbulent 1960s. Demonstrations were frequent and the area was a center of hippie culture.

Today it's more of a carnival than a riot. During the daytime, the avenue is thickly lined with street vendors, hawking clothes, jewelry, and other articles of adornment. Smokeshop **Annapurna** (No. 2416, www.annapurnaberkeley.com) is a reminder of the area's hippie past. There are many quality bookstores including **Cody's Books** (No. 2454, www.codysbooks.com), which hosts readings by big name authors, and **Moe's** (No. 2476, www.moesbooks.com), beloved for its used books. At night, the street is the setting for a lively collegiate party. Of the many cheap eateries and bars, the best known are **Blondie's Pizza** (No. 2340) and **Blake's** (No. 2367, www.blakesontelegraph.com).

Rockridge *the other gourmet ghetto*
College Avenue, Oakland;
BART to Rockridge Station

Rockridge is a green, residential area known for the food shops on College Avenue. Culturally this is part of Berkeley, where the more famous Gourmet Ghetto *(see p47)* lies; the only sign that College Avenue has crossed from one city to the other being the change in police badges. The hub of this land of excellent taste is found at the **Market Hall** (No. 5655, www.rockridge markethall.com), which sells a wide variety of foods from all over the world, and the adjacent **Oliveto** (No. 5655, www.oliveto.com), a restaurant offering Tuscan treats. Nearby **Nan Yang** (No. 6048) is the best (and only) Burmese restaurant in the East Bay. For a table full of French-inspired small plates in a festive atmosphere try A Côté (No. 5478, *see p47*). It's usually packed, so go early or late. The other regional specialty here is used goods: visit **Rockridge Rags** (No. 5711) for high-quality vintage clothing and accessories.

havens

In this compact city of hills, peace is never far away. There are over 200 public parks, and myriad sea views from rooftops and grassy bluffs above the Pacific. Not far from the rush of the Financial District and the bustle of Chinatown, you will find refuge in tearooms, spas, and quiet gardens. For an energizing blast of salt air, hop on a ferry to the wildlands across the Bay.

Havens

Embarcadero Center Terrace `2 F4`

Justin Herman Plaza • 800 733 6318
>> www.embarcaderocenter.com
Open 10–7 Mon–Fri, 10–6 Sat, noon–5 Sun

The Promenade on the upper levels of this shopping complex is a lovely spot from which to admire fantastic views of the Bay. The series of interconnected terrace gardens and elevated walkways are accessed by elevator from Embarcadero Center 4.

Bay Ferries *cruises across the Bay* `1 D1`

Ticket offices at Pier 39 and Pier 41 • 415 705 8200
>> www.blueandgoldfleet.com See website for schedules

Take to the water for some fresh air and some of the best views of the Golden Gate Bridge *(see p12)* and the city's historic waterfront on Blue and Gold Fleet's hour-long San Francisco Bay Cruise. Ferry services to the seaside towns of Sausalito and Tiburon depart from Pier 41 and offer refreshments on board.

Imperial Tea Court *a calming cup* `1 D4`

1411 Powell Street • 415 788 6080
>> www.imperialtea.com Open 11–6:30 Wed–Mon

This traditional Chinese teahouse is a red-and-gold daydream, complete with hanging birdcages, glowing lanterns, and gleaming mahogany furnishings. Located away from the rush of Chinatown, Imperial Tea offers a wide range of rare and specialty teas, as well as formal Gong Fu Tea Presentations.

Chair Massage

After a fast-paced day, a chair massage works wonders for tension in the shoulders, neck, and back. The experienced therapists at the super-hip **Elephant Pharmacy** (1607 Shattuck Avenue, 510 549 9200, www.elephantpharmacy.com), in Berkeley, are experts at stress relief. The pharmacy also stocks a range of alternative health and beauty products.

Pharmaca (Map 10 F3, 925 Cole St., 415 661 1216, www.pharmaca.com/events_cole.html) is a pharmacy and drugstore with Acupressure Chair Massage every Saturday 1–6pm, at $1 per minute. On 20th Avenue, **Sunset Sauna and Massage** (Map 9 B3, 415 753 2559, www.sunsetsauna.com) offers soothing sessions. Prices start from $9.95 for 10 minutes, and you can linger in the leafy garden.

For the very latest on San Francisco go to >> **www.realcity.dk.com**

Nob Hill Spa *swim, steam, work out* `1 D5`

Huntington Hotel, 1075 California Street • 415 345 2888
>> www.huntingtonhotel.com Open 7:30am–9pm daily

Cloistered within the Huntington Hotel *(see p151)*, one of the city's most opulent small hotels and a favorite of royals and celebrities, is a two-story, glass-walled atrium where spa guests can swim in an infinity pool and gaze out at the downtown skyline.

The environment, designed by a feng shui consultant, is formal, yet sensuous and soothing. The lobby area is decorated in pale gray-green with gold mosaic ribbons, and a sweeping spiral staircase curves down past the pool. Oversize chairs by the fireplaces make cozy retreats on foggy days; when the sun comes out, visitors can relax on chaise lounges on the patio.

There are ten plush treatment rooms with rose-petal-covered tables where visitors can experience one of the many body treatments, facials, and massages on offer. Try the Bali Ginger Spice Scrub; or the Asian-inspired "ScenTao" treatment designed to unblock Qi flow – a full body aromatherapy scrub with exotic plant extracts to soften the skin, followed by a heated stone massage, and rounded off with an enlivening cup of green tea and an aromatic facial.

Spa cuisine is prepared in the hotel's legendary Big Four Restaurant and served poolside. The menu includes healthy treats such as passion fruit, wild berry, and ginseng smoothies, and dishes like Dungeness crab cakes with crispy artichoke. Other facilities in this pleasure palace include a eucalyptus steam room, indoor pool, weight-training venue, and classes in yoga and Pilates. Entry is free for hotel guests or with a spa treatment; otherwise a day pass (Mon–Thu) costs $35.

>> *Imperial Tea Court also has a branch in the Ferry Building Marketplace* (see p52)

Havens

SF Art Institute Café *a quiet lunch* `1 C2`
800 Chestnut Street • 415 749 4567
» www.sfai.edu Open 8–5 Mon–Thu, 8–4 Fri

This Spanish-style courtyard café is well away from the fray, on the rooftop of the city's oldest art school. Enjoy panoramic views of the Bay with an espresso or an inexpensive breakfast or lunch. While you're here, take the opportunity to see the monumental 1931 mural in the Diego Rivera Gallery.

Marina Green *picnic on the grass* `8 G1`
Marina Boulevard bet. Scott and Webster Sts. • 415 831 2700
Open daylight hours

The Marina Green is San Francisco's front yard, a vast greensward running along the waterfront. A spectacular display of kites is guaranteed here every windy weekend and, with unobstructed views of the Bay, the bridge, and the Marin Headlands, it's the perfect spot for a leisurely picnic or a stroll.

International Orange Spa *super spa* `8 H4`
2044 Fillmore Street • 415 563 5000
» www.internationalorange.com Spa services: 11–9 Mon–Fri, 9–7 Sat & Sun; yoga classes offered daily, call for schedules

A chic, airy bubble of spa experiences and yoga classes. The nourishing In Fiore range of body balms are used for massages and the "Red Flower Japan" exfoliation treatment. Included in the amenities are a lounge with fireplace, and a beautiful redwood sundeck.

Small Parks and Hideaways
San Francisco has plenty of small parks and quiet spaces. Tiny **Huntington Park** (Map 1 D5, nobhill association.org) atop Nob Hill is the choice of the stylish set. Look out for the replica of Rome's curvaceous Tartarughe Fountain. Across the street, **Grace Cathedral** *(see p71)* has two labyrinths designed for a meditative stroll, one outside on the terrazzo stone floor and the other indoors below the glorious rose window. The steep **Filbert Steps** (Map 2 E3) ascend Telegraph Hill past gardens and pretty clapboard cottages. **Redwood Park** (Map 2 F4) is a half-acre patch of green at the foot of the city's iconic 48-story Transamerica Pyramid where office workers lunch. Across town, **Alta Plaza Park** (Map 8 G3) rises in landscaped terraces above Pacific Heights.

Wilderness Across the Bridge

The wild open spaces of Marin County lure bikers, hikers, and beachcombers north across the Golden Gate Bridge. Below the hillside trails of the **Marin Headlands** (www.nps.gov/goga/mahe), a rugged coastline shelters small beaches and Point Bonita Lighthouse. **Point Reyes National Seashore** (415 464 5100, www.nps.gov/pore) consists of thousands of acres of wildflower meadows, forest glens, and blustery beaches. Marin County is dominated by **Mount Tamalpais** (415 388 2070, www.mttam.net), a 2,500-ft (760-m) peak threaded with trails, waterfall canyons, and streambeds. At its foot, **Muir Woods National Monument** (415 388 2595, www.nps.gov/muwo) is a silent, misty grove of California coastal redwoods.

Kabuki Springs & Spa *soak and scrub* `8 H5`
1750 Geary Boulevard • 415 922 6000
>> www.kabukisprings.com Open 10–9:45 daily

This authentic Japanese communal bathhouse is open to men (Mon, Thu, Sat) and women (Sun, Wed, Fri) – Tuesdays are co-ed but you'll be required to wear a bathing suit. There's a steam room and dry sauna, cold pool, and hot tub, and bathers can follow their dip with a Shiatsu "finger pressure" massage or a body wrap.

SF Zen Center *morning meditation* `3 A4`
300 Page Street • 415 863 3136
>> www.sfzc.org Office open 9:30–4 Mon–Fri, 8:30–noon Sat

The Zen Center – also called the "Beginner's Mind Temple" – is housed in a Craftsman-style 1920s architectural landmark designed by Julia Morgan *(see p83)*. For over three decades it has been a meeting place for the large community of San Franciscans who practice Zen Buddhism; visitors are also welcome.

The Saturday morning introduction to meditation and Buddhism (arrive by 8:30am) takes place in a serene, welcoming setting. No registration is required and you can come as many times as you wish. Tea and a healthy lunch are served afterwards, for a small fee.

The center holds daily sitting and walking meditation practice periods and hosts speakers on Buddhist practice, philosophy, and history. There is also a specialized library and a bookstore. The Marin County annex, Green Gulch Farm, is located in a verdant valley and offers popular Sunday tea gatherings.

>> *After meditation at the SF Zen Center, have a bowl of soup at cozy Kate's Kitchen (471 Haight Street)*

Havens

Crissy Field *seaside sanctuary* 7 D1
Old Mason Street at Marina Boulevard • 415 561 7690
>> www.crissyfield.org Open daylight hours

On the shoreline below the Golden Gate Bridge, Crissy Field is a grassy open space made up of small sandy beaches, marshlands, and a meadow. There are paved footpaths across the 100-acre (40-ha) site, and the salt air makes it a very refreshing place for a walk.

The restored marshlands and dunes are home to an array of wildlife and plants. Bird-watchers flock here to see migrating and resident feathered creatures – herons, grebes, willets, and killdeer. On display at the Gulf of the Farallones Marine Sanctuary Visitors' Center are exhibits of great white sharks and other sea life.

The Warming Hut café and bookstore and the Crissy Field Center café offer shelter and hot drinks when the fog drifts in. From the Warming Hut walk along to Torpedo Wharf to watch the fishermen, and then on to Civil War-era Fort Point National Historic Site, under the bridge, to see the museum, guns, and cannons.

Angel Island State Park *island retreat*
Ferry departs from Pier 41 (Map 1 D1) • 415 705 5555
>> www.blueandgoldfleet.com
Angel Island: 415 435 3522
>> www.angelisland.org Open 8am–sunset all year round

This hilly, wooded island lies across the Bay, just south of the Tiburon peninsula and a half-hour ferry ride from Fisherman's Wharf. By the dock there are lawns for lounging and picnicking, and you can watch the sea birds and yachts glide by.

The hour-long narrated tram ride (Mar–late Nov, ticket office at the Cove Café) is a good way to tour the vestiges of the island's lively history, which include an ancient Miwok settlement and historic immigration stations. The tram stops at vantage points for photo opportunities. More energetic visitors can explore the island on a naturalist-guided sea kayak tour (415 488 1000), and there are miles of trails for hiking and mountain biking; bikes can be brought over on the ferry or rented on arrival.

Yerba Buena Gardens *midtown green* **4 F2**

Mission Street between 3rd and 4th Streets • 415 541 0312

>> www.yerbabuenagardens.com Open 6am–10pm daily

This sprawling, green breathing space in the SoMa district is the city's backyard. Sweeping lawns and blooming gardens contain outdoor sculpture, while a woodland grove and soothing water features create an atmosphere of serenity. From the upper terraces, the 360-degree panorama is of high-rise hotels, historic churches, major museums, and a looming, glass-walled entertainment center, Metreon *(see p62)*.

Cascades and a waterfall block traffic noise for city-weary lunchtimers and afternoon loungers, who are treated to occasional live concerts. You can sit in an outdoor café overlooking the trees, or have lunch on the lawn under the sycamores and, in the spring, the pink-flowering cherry trees. If you can rouse yourself from a prone position on the grassy esplanade, explore the nearby Yerba Buena Center for the Arts *(see pp74 and 97)*, and, across the street, the soaring, modernist SFMOMA *(see p78)*. Among a plethora of art features in the gardens is a 50-ft (15-m) wide wall of water which drops in a torrent, creating a grotto in which excerpts from Martin Luther King, Jr.'s "I Have a Dream" speech are engraved on glass panels.

A serene oasis on weekdays, the Gardens are busy with free performances and festivals on weekends from May to October, from Latin jazz concerts to art displays, opera and symphony, literary and spoken-word events, and the San Francisco Theater Festival on nine indoor and outdoor stages. Accessed by elevated walkway above the gardens, the glass-enclosed Yerba Buena Ice Skating Center welcomes visitors to watch the skaters and hockey players.

Havens

Golden Gate Park *a green oasis* `11 C4`

Park Headquarters: 501 Stanyan Street • 415 831 2700
Visitors' Center located in The Beach Chalet • 415 751 2766
» www.parks.sfgov.org Open daylight hours

This glorious retreat from city life stretches from the Haight-Ashbury district to the Pacific in a wide swath of meadows, hills, forests, and flower gardens. Among the innumerable attractions are a boating lake, tennis courts, and baseball diamonds. Tulips bloom around the Dutch windmill to the west of the park, and the Golden Gate Park Band (www.goldengateparkband.org) gives free outdoor concerts in the Music Concourse every Sunday, April–October. On Sundays the main road, JFK Drive, is closed to vehicles for Rollerblading, cycling, skateboarding, and jogging. Parking is difficult on weekends; shuttle buses will scoot you around.

The **Conservatory of Flowers** (Map 9 D2, www. conservatoryofflowers.org, open 9–4:30 Tue–Sun) makes a warm refuge on a foggy day in the park. A monumental glass greenhouse which was crafted in Dublin and shipped around Cape Horn in the 1870s, it is like a Victorian biosphere, sheltering a steamy, dreamy, five-story jungle of trees, exotic plants, and flowers. Leaves as big as Hummers, lily ponds, Tarzan vines, gorgeous orchids, and fragrant, blooming bulbs are among the sights.

The **San Francisco Botanical Garden at Strybing Arboretum** (Map 9 C2, www.sfbotanicalgarden.org, open 8–4:30 Mon–Fri, 10–5 Sat & Sun) is home to an array of birds and waterfowl. There are themed gardens from the Mediterranean, Australia, and South America, and an enchanting cloud forest where you

will find solitude even on busy weekends. In the redwood grove there's a rare Dawn Redwood from China. The fragrance garden is planted with sweet-smelling herbs, and the Moon-Viewing Garden is home to the largest stone lantern outside Japan.

The oldest public Japanese garden in America, the **Japanese Tea Garden** (Map 9 C2, open 8:30–6 daily) is a fantasy of cherry trees, dark pines, and lily ponds swimming with golden carp. Its bronze Buddha was cast in 1790 in Japan and, along with the gilded five-level pagoda, is a favorite backdrop for photos. In April, cherry blossoms form a fragrant white cloud, and the rhododendrons are oceans of magenta, pink, and white; in fall, maples blaze red and gold. Jasmine tea and fortune cookies are served by kimono-clad women in the open-air café.

The **National AIDS Memorial Grove** (Map 9 D2, www. aidsmemorial.org) is a serene dell of towering redwoods and pines. In the spring, white dogwood blooms around the Circle of Friends, where the names of those touched by and lost to AIDS are inscribed on the flagstone floor; look for the names of Robin Williams and Sharon Stone honoring their loved ones.

From a window table at the **Beach Chalet Brewery and Restaurant** *(see p82,* Map 11 A4, www.beach chalet.com), you can watch the sun set over Ocean Beach. Microbrews, seafood, and hearty pub fare are on the menu in this terra-cotta-tiled 1925 architectural masterpiece by Willis Polk. Out back, the Park Chalet is a casual, light-filled café with a stone fireplace, a window wall open on warm days, and chairs on the lawn fronting the park.

hotels

This is a city brimming with inviting accommodation. It makes sense that the "boutique" hotel concept got its start in San Francisco: a property has to stand out to attract attention and must pamper its guests to ensure their return. Whether you stay in a charming inn off the beaten path or a five-star palace in the heart of town, you can be sure of a warm welcome and high standards of service.

HOTELS

The Internet has transformed travel, making it easy to reserve accommodations in San Francisco online, often at greatly reduced rates. You'll also nearly always get a discount if you use a reservation service (my favorite is www. cheaphotels.co.uk). That said, you can always try asking any hotel, whether a charming off-the-beaten-path inn or a hip, urbane hostelry, to reduce its rates or to match an online offer. You can *always* improve on the rack rate.

Peter Cieply

Groovy Rooms

For far-out West Coast style, check into the **Hotel del Sol** *(see p157)*, where palm trees and beach-stripe decor evoke SoCal beach towns. Or try the **Triton** *(see p154)*, with its celebrity-designed suites and funky attitude. Alternatively, the trendy **Phoenix Hotel** *(see p154)* is arranged around a faux-tropical courtyard and attracts party people and rock stars.

Spas and Sports

Several SF hotels offer more than just a room for some real R&R. The **Huntington Hotel** *(see p151)* is home to the superlative Nob Hill Spa, while the **Hotel Vitale** *(see p159)* capitalizes on it its bayfront setting with rooftop soaking tubs. The **Four Seasons San Francisco** *(see p152)* ups the ante with its ultra-chic Sports Club LA and a spa.

Peace, Quiet, and Privacy

If out-of-the-way is how you like to stay, you'll appreciate the tranquil site and upscale discretion of the **Hotel Drisco** *(see p158)* – choice of some celebrities. Nearby, the **Jackson Court Hotel** *(see p158)*, a stately brownstone, is an upscale B&B and a real haven. The Edwardian **Hotel Majestic** *(see p156)* also exudes calm and offers romantic rooms.

choice stays

Great Views

Certain hotels offer some of the best views in town. Guests have visited the **InterContinental Mark Hopkins** *(see p153)* since 1926 to watch the sun set from its top-floor lounge bar, and the **Park Hyatt**'s *(see p150)* balcony rooms are very impressive. If you'd like to gaze upon the Bay Bridge from your room, check into the intimate **Hotel Griffon** *(see p159)*.

Style Statements

Stylish rooms don't have to cost a fortune. Contemporary decor and a hot in-house restaurant help attract a loyal clientele at the **Hotel Adagio** *(see p155)*, while a hip bar and modern design earn laurels for the **Laurel Inn** *(see p156)*. For a splurge, stay at the **St. Regis San Francisco** *(see p158)*, with luxurious bathrooms that open out into the rooms.

Best of the Boutiques

For unique hotels with amenities to match, look to the health-conscious **Nob Hill Lambourne** *(see p152)*, where you get vitamins on your pillow at night; the prestigious **Prescott** *(see p155)*, whose in-house restaurant is no less than Wolfgang Puck's Postrio; or the whimsical **Hotel Monaco** *(see p150)*, which offers tarot readings, massages, and pet goldfish.

Hotel Monaco *Theater District panache*

501 Geary Street • 415 292 0100
>> www.monaco-sf.com

This downtown, boutique gem is a whimsical, stylish conversion of a 1910 Beaux-Arts hotel. Amenities are top-flight, with canopy beds, Frette bathrobes, and a complimentary nightly wine reception with tarot card reading and chair massage. You can even get a pet goldfish for the duration of your stay. **Moderate**

Park Hyatt *stylish business accommodation* 2 F4

333 Battery Street • 415 392 1234
>> www.parksanfrancisco.hyatt.com

You don't have to be in town on business to enjoy this elegant hotel in the center of the Financial District. Most rooms have great city or Bay views, and many have balconies. Standard rooms are spacious, and basic amenities include large-screen TVs, cordless phones, and goosedown duvets. **Expensive**

Omni San Francisco *1920s elegance* 2 E5

500 California Street • 415 677 9494
>> www.omnisanfrancisco.com

This first-class hotel in the heart of the Financial District scores high marks for comfort and excellent service. Housed in a restored 1926 office building, the Omni has kept the 1920s aesthetic (crown moldings, cherry wood, patterned fabrics) but added all the modern amenities. **Expensive**

Online Reservation Services

There are countless hotel reservation agencies where you can sometimes find great discounts on room rates, and San Francisco has a couple of good homegrown options. **San Francisco Reservations** (510 628 4450, www.hotelres.com) helps you find a room at one of nearly 300 hotels in the area, frequently at a discounted rate. Unlike many hotel agencies, they don't charge fees, even for cancellations (unless you opt for a "contract rate," which guarantees a discount but you must pay in full upfront). The **San Francisco Convention & Visitors Bureau Official Citywide Hotel Reservation Service** (800 637 5196, www.sfvisitor.org) offers phone or online reservation often with no service fee. Most prices offered are discounted Internet rates.

Huntington Hotel *heights of discretion* 1 D5

1075 California Street • 415 474 5400

>> www.huntingtonhotel.com

This stately Georgian-style building was the first steel-and-brick high-rise built west of the Mississippi River. Situated on Nob Hill, it faces beautiful Grace Cathedral *(see p71)* and the Flood Mansion (now the exclusive Pacific-Union Club). Ever since it was converted from an elite apartment building in 1945, it has been first choice for accommodation in the city, and has hosted such luminaries as the Vanderbilts, Bogart and Bacall, Princess Grace, and Prince Charles.

A distinguished family-run hotel, the Huntington is known for its discreet, personalized service and tastefully elegant decor, as well as for its superlative Nob Hill Spa *(see p139)*. Rooms are unusually spacious since they were originally built as apartments, and – because of the hotel's setting – all have great views of either the city or Huntington Park *(see p140)* and the cathedral. All the rooms and suites are individually designed, and many contain rare and original artworks.

Guests are greeted with complimentary in-room formal tea or sherry service, which sets the tone for a stay here. Amenities and services are all first-rate and up-to-date, including complimentary use of the Spa, high-speed Internet access, chauffered sedan service to the Financial District and Union Square, and a laundry and twice-daily maid service, among many other pleasant perks.

Off the lobby, the Big 4 Restaurant and lounge is a handsome, clubby getaway, named for the "big four" 19th-century railroad tycoons who lived in mansion atop Nob Hill. Its superlative American cuisine is as popular with well-heeled locals as it is with hotel guests, and the dining room showcases an interesting collection of 19th-century railroad and early California memorabilia.

At your doorstep, the California Street cable cars (less frequented by tourists and therefore easier and more fun to ride) rumble right past the hotel, and across the street, Huntington Park hosts morning tai chi practitioners and afternoon picnickers. **Expensive**

>> *Cheap: up to $150 for a double room; moderate: $150–300; expensive: over $300*

Hotels

Nob Hill Lambourne *healthy alternative* `2 E5`
725 Pine Street • 415 433 2287
>> www.nobhilllambourne.com

This small, comfortable hotel offers simple, elegant decor and unusual amenities for high-powered and health-conscious types. These include yoga videos and equipment, Asian-inspired massage treatments, all-natural bath products, and a mini-bar stocked with organic products. **Moderate**

Ritz-Carlton San Francisco *new tricks* `2 E5`
600 Stockton Street • 415 296 7465
>> www.ritzcarlton.com/hotels/san_francisco

This Neoclassical Nob Hill temple is the only five-star/five-diamond hotel and restaurant in North America. It offers everything you'd expect from a Ritz – right down to providing "Nanny survival kits" for your au pair and an on-call "technology butler" who will fix your computer glitches. **Expensive**

Four Seasons San Francisco `4 E1`
757 Market Street • 415 633 3000
>> www.fourseasons.com/sanfrancisco

Despite its address on an unprepossessing downtown stretch of Market Street, the Four Seasons is one of the most luxurious hotels in the city. Occupying 12 levels of the Four Seasons apartment tower, the hotel's rooms and common areas carry through the ambience of an upmarket modern residence, with an outstanding collection of contemporary Northern California art peppered throughout. The ultra-chic on-site Sports Club/LA provides a gym, a spa, and a junior Olympic swimming pool, and access is free for hotel guests.

All 277 rooms and suites are generous – the city's largest, at 460 sq ft (42.7 sq m) minimum. The floor-to-ceiling windows open for air and offer great city and East Bay views. Less expensive rooms, on the 6th and 7th floors, have more obstructions; on these floors, ask for a central room looking straight out over Grant Avenue toward the Chinatown Gate. **Expensive**

Campton Place *personal attention*

`4 E1`

340 Stockton Street • 415 781 5555
>> www.camptonplace.com

With its clean-lined decor and air of understated elegance, Campton Place is an oasis in the heart of downtown. Just steps off Union Square, it's perfect for decamping to after a shopping spree on Maiden Lane *(see p55)*. There are 110 rooms and suites, and everyone is catered to personally, down to the freshly-baked cookie placed bedside at turndown.

Rooms are spacious and individually decorated, with an Asian-inflected mix of Old World and sleek contemporary furnishings, cotton sheets, down duvets, limestone-tiled bathrooms, and capacious closets. There's a unique tented rooftop fitness terrace overlooking Union Square, and the house restaurant is one of the city's finest hotel dining rooms. Amenities include 24-hour room service, high-speed Internet connections, video on-demand, and custom bath products. Pets are welcome, too. **Expensive**

The Old Guard

San Francisco is a great hotel city, with more than its share of classics. Staying in one of these grand old dames is a step back into the city's past. Visitors seem to love the famous Beefeater-costumed doorman at the historic 1928 **Sir Francis Drake** (Map 2 E5, 450 Powell St., 415 392 7755, www.sirfrancis drake.com). This city landmark got a "boutique hotel" update in the 1990s and now boasts bold colors, contemporary design, and plush amenities. Its opulent top-floor Starlight Room nightclub *(see p108)* has panoramic views and an old-fashioned glamour.

Right on Union Square, the majestic **Westin St. Francis** (Map 4 E1, 335 Powell St., 415 397 7000, www.westinstfrancis.com) has been the place for San Franciscans to meet since 1904. Attention to detail at this hotel extends as far as the washing of all coin money used here, a tradition originally born of not wanting to soil ladies' gloves.

The **Fairmont San Francisco** (Map 1 D5, 950 Mason St., 415 772 5000, www.fairmont.com/sanfrancisco) literally rose from the ashes of the 1906 earthquake and fire – it opened a year later, fully restored by the nation's first woman architect, Julia Morgan. Tony Bennett first sang "I Left My Heart..." in its Venetian Room lounge. The **InterContinental Mark Hopkins Hotel** (Map 1 D5, 999 California St., 415 392 3434, www.san-francisco.intercontinental.com) gets mentioned in another classic song, "San Francisco"; you can still "watch it get dark from the Top of the Mark," its famous lounge *(see p107)* atop Nob Hill.

The grand old **Palace Hotel** (Map 4 F1, 2 New Montgomery St., 415 512 1111, www.sfpalace.com) has many tales to tell, one of the more intriguing being the mysterious death of President Warren G. Harding here, in the company of a woman not his wife. The hotel's central Garden Court is recognized as one of the world's most splendid public spaces.

Phoenix Hotel *rock'n'roll hot spot* `3 C2`

601 Eddy Street • 415 776 1380
>> www.thephoenixhotel.com

SF meets LA at this hypertrendy motel-turned-rock-star-hangout on a gritty block of the Tenderloin district. Forty-one guestrooms and three suites open out onto a surreal faux-tropical courtyard and sculpture garden complete with palm trees and a heated swimming pool. Sure, someone may be shooting up on the street out front, but in the courtyard you might be hanging with Pearl Jam, sipping cocktails from the groovy in-house Bambuddha Lounge *(see p109)* and laughing about the last time you were here talking to David Bowie.

   This bijou oasis is centrally located and very reasonably priced, offering amenities like concierge, valet and laundry services, poolside continental breakfast, and free parking (even if you're parking a tour bus). Be aware that this is a place for party people, and nighttime presents just two options: party along or bring earplugs. **Cheap**

Hotel Rex *salon-style hospitality* `3 D1`

562 Sutter Street • 415 433 4434
>> www.thehotelrex.com

The estimable Joie de Vivre company likes to think of a magazine when coming up with the style of a property. This one is inspired by *The New Yorker* and the literary salons of the 1920s and 30s. It has a warm, bookish, clubby feel, with many original 1930s portraits and drawings on the walls. **Cheap**

Hotel Triton *star-studded suites* `2 E5`

342 Grant Avenue • 415 394 0500
>> www.hoteltriton.com

This hip boutique hotel at the Chinatown Gateway exudes a naughty-goofy glamour with its "Sex in the City" package. Among the celebrity-designed suites is a "Red Hot Love Nest" decorated with Chili Pepper memorabilia, and a Jerry Garcia room. There's a complimentary wine reception every night. **Moderate**

Commodore Hotel *red-hot residence*

3 D1

825 Sutter Street • 415 923 6800
>> www.thecommodorehotel.com

This hipster hot spot is best known locally for its Red Room bar *(see p109)*, but that's not actually the most colorful part of the place. The decor throughout riffs on a 1920s ocean liner, using a lively palette of high-voltage color. Amenities are standard-plus and include dataports and cable TV with pay-per-view. **Cheap**

Prescott Hotel *gourmet luxury*

3 D1

545 Post Street • 415 563 0303
>> www.prescotthotel.com

The rooms at this sophisticated boutique hotel are smallish but smart, with custom-designed cherry furniture and richly hued Lauren fabrics. "Club Level" guests have use of the concierge-staffed lounge, and the in-house restaurant is chef Wolfgang Puck's award-winning Postrio. **Moderate**

Hotel Adagio *modern pizzazz*

3 D1

550 Geary Street • 415 775 5000
>> www.thehoteladagio.com

This 1929 Spanish Colonial Revival building got an $11 million facelift in 2003 from the Joie de Vivre hospitality group, whose boutique hotels offer some of the best value in the city.

Now, with its sharply stylish Barcelona-mod decor, 171 spacious, reasonably priced rooms, and popular in-house restaurant, Cortez *(see p29)*, it's a great choice for a downtown hotel. It's located right in the heart of the Theater District, close to business and shopping destinations, and a complimentary morning town car service is available. All rooms are quiet, with high-speed Internet access, CD players, Sony Wega TVs with pay-per-view movies and games, cordless speakerphones with voicemail, and Aveda bath products. Ask for the 01 or 04 series rooms for the best views and bay windows, or splurge on the Bolero Suite with its outdoor terrace. **Moderate**

Hotel Bohème *Beat Generation charmer* `2 E3`

444 Columbus Avenue • 415 433 9111
>> www.hotelboheme.com

A hip Euro-bohemian hotel that fits right into North Beach, the most European of the city's neighborhoods and the original home of the Beat poets. The black-and-jewel-tone retro decor exudes an arty spirit, and the 15 rooms are romantically cozy and up-to-date, with WiFi connection throughout. **Moderate**

Hotel Majestic *Old World elegance* `3 B1`

1500 Sutter Street • 415 441 1100
>> www.thehotelmajestic.com

This Edwardian mansion has operated as a hotel since 1904 (the 1906 fires stopped blocks away) and was once a permanent home to screen siren Joan Fontaine. It retains the feel of a film set, all English and French antiques and patterned carpets. WiFi and other amenities bring it up-to-date. **Cheap**

Laurel Inn *hip neighborhood hangout* `8 F4`

444 Presidio Avenue • 415 567 8467
>> www.thelaurelinn.com

This renovated 1960s hotel adopts a fresh take on Mid-Century Modern design in its studio-apartment-style rooms. Many have stunning views of the city, and 18 include kitchenettes. Chic shops and restaurants line the nearby streets, and the hotel's G-Bar is a favorite hipster watering hole. **Moderate**

Motel Capri *unbelievable bargain* `8 H2`

2015 Greenwich Street
415 346 4667

It's not stylish by any means, unless you like your 1960s style straight up: nothing has changed at this quintessential motor lodge since then (the brochure at the front desk looks like a camp collectible). But it is immaculately clean, located near many happening areas, and it even has free parking. **Cheap**

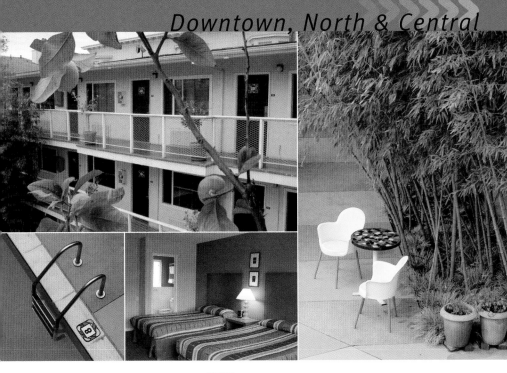

Hotel del Sol *fun in the sun*

`8 H2`

3100 Webster Street • 415 921 5520

>> www.thehoteldelsol.com

When the Joie de Vivre hotel folks revamped this 1950s Marina District motor lodge, they were clearly in a trippy "California Dreamin" frame of mind. The property sports a southern California aesthetic, but kicks it up a couple of notches – there is eye-popping color everywhere, from the lemon-yellow walls and cobalt-blue terrazzo tables to the cabana-stripe fabric garage "doors" on the parking bays. The hotel's centerpiece is a huge courtyard with towering palms, stands of bamboo, and a heated pool (maintained at a balmy 78–82°F). In this "cool gray city of love," stepping off the street into this hot resort setting is a through-the-looking-glass experience.

Indoors, a playfully stylish decor prevails, with more beach stripes and bold colors and designs. Standard rooms are large, with roomy closets,

wireless Internet connections, two-line phones with voicemail and dataports, CD and VCR players, and cable television. Other amenities include a concierge service, continental breakfast served poolside, Aveda bath products, laundry and valet services, and a video lending library. Some of the 10 suites have kitchenettes, and two have fireplaces.

Parking is included in the room price, an almost unheard-of luxury, especially given the reasonable rates. But you don't need a car to get to some of the city's liveliest areas from here. It's a short walk to Chestnut, Union, and upper Fillmore streets – good news for folks looking for nightlife and singles' spots or charming and chic restaurants and shops. For those looking for peace and quiet, it's also a pleasant stroll down to the Marina Green *(see p140)*, the Palace of Fine Arts *(see p73)*, and Crissy Field *(see p142)*, where you can continue California dreamin' with a picnic on the beach, gazing out at the Golden Gate. **Cheap**

>> *Avoid the lower-end chain hotels; many boutique hotels are much nicer and just as affordable*

W San Francisco *style and service*   `4 F2`

181 3rd Street • 415 777 5300

>> www.starwoodhotels.com/whotels

The sleek and savvy W hotel folks know how to create a scene as well as they know how to care for guests. The DJ-driven lounge bar XYZ is hopping most nights with a hip mix of locals and visitors, and the company's "whatever/whenever service" guarantees that guests get most everything they desire. **Expensive**

St. Regis San Francisco *ultra luxury*   `4 F1`

125 3rd Street • 415 284 4000

>> www.starwoodhotels.com/stregis

The St. Regis chain positions itself as the leader of luxe, and with its sumptuous "residence-style" rooms tricked out with all the latest technology and the hotel's legendary butler service, who can argue? Baths have shutters that open out onto the room, so you can enjoy the views from the deep-soaking tub. **Expensive**

Room at the Inn

Inns in San Francisco are an attractive alternative to hotels and offer the feeling of being a resident of a city neighborhood. Unlike many B&B, where an abundance of teddy bears and floral prints can be mildy nauseating, these gracious old mansions and converted apartment buildings are sophisticated, not saccharine. Smaller and cozier than hotels, they offer many of the same amenities, like WiFi or data ports. Cost ranges from moderate to moderately expensive, depending upon how upscale you want to go.

For an over-the-top experience, stay on Alamo Square in one of the opulent opera-named rooms at the **Archbishop's Mansion** (Map 10 H1, 1000 Fulton St., 415 563 7872, www.thearchbishops mansion.com). Decorated to replicate a French *belle époque* mansion, its furnishings include a grand piano once owned by Noel Coward and a chandelier used in the film *Gone With the Wind*.

Alternatively, head up to Pacific Heights, home to two handsome inn-hotels. The elegant **Hotel Drisco** (Map 8 G3, 2901 Pacific Ave., 415 929 7670, www. hoteldrisco.com) has some rooms with Bay views and occasionally hosts celebrities who want to stay out of the public eye. Stately **Jackson Court** (Map 8 H3, 2198 Jackson St., 800 738 7477, www.jackson court.com) is a 19th-century brownstone just a stone's throw from trendy upper Fillmore Street.

If you want to stay in a classic Victorian "painted lady" mansion, make your way to the **Stanyan Park Hotel** (Map 10 E2, 750 Stanyan St., 415 751 1000, www.stanyanpark.com). It overlooks Golden Gate Park and is listed on the National Register of Historic Places. The charming **Washington Square Inn** (Map 1 D3, 1660 Stockton St., 415 981 4220, www.wsi sf.com) is located in the heart of North Beach *(see pp126–7)* and has views over Washington Square park and the Saints Peter and Paul Church.

Harbor Court Hotel *Bay-front boutique* `2 G5`
165 Steuart Street • 415 882 1300
>> www.harborcourthotel.com

This former YMCA once housed soldiers in bunk beds, but now it's a comfortable boutique hotel with great Bay views. Amenities are state-of-the-art, including WiFi and on-demand movies. Guests can use the YMCA health club and pool next door, and room service is from the terrific sushi restaurant, Ozumo. **Moderate**

Hotel Vitale *luxury lodgings by the Bay* `2 G4`
8 Mission Street • 415 278 3700
>> www.hotelvitale.com

This deluxe spa hotel on the Embarcadero waterfront makes the most of its site, offering rooftop soaking tubs and circular suites with 270-degree Bay views. The decor is fresh and contemporary, and famous local restaurateur Pascal Rigo provides room service from his new Americano restaurant. **Expensive**

Hotel Griffon *cool and contemporary* `2 G5`
155 Steuart Street • 415 495 2100
>> www.hotelgriffon.com

A favorite of business travelers looking for a more personal touch, the Griffon is a handsomely furnished hotel whose best features are its personal service (the bellman runs errands) and great location on the Embarcadero. Six of the rooms and five suites look directly out at the Bay Bridge. **Moderate**

Seal Rock Inn *get away from it all* `11 A2`
545 Point Lobos Avenue • 415 752 8000
>> www.sealrockinn.com

Staying here feels like landing in a small beach town in the 1960s. The inn overlooks Sutro Heights Park and the ocean, it's a short stroll to the Cliff House *(see p45)* and Ocean Beach, and there's a patio with a pool, ping-pong, and badminton. The decor is dated, but it's very clean and parking is free. **Cheap**

San Francisco Street Finder

Almost every listing in this guide includes a page and grid reference to the maps in this Street Finder section. The few entries that fall outside the area covered by these maps have transport details instead. The main map below shows the divisions of the Street Finder, and the smaller one to the right shows the extent of the Bay Area.

Key to Street Finder

- Sight/public building
- 🅑 BART station
- 🄲 Caltrain station
- Ⓜ Muni Metro station
- 🚌 Bus terminal
- ⛴ Ferry boarding point
- ℹ Tourist information office
- ⊕ Hospital with casualty unit
- Police station
- Church
- Synagogue
- Mosque
- ⊗ Post office
- Golf course
- Cable car terminal
- Cable car route
- Pedestrian street
- Railroad line
- Freeway

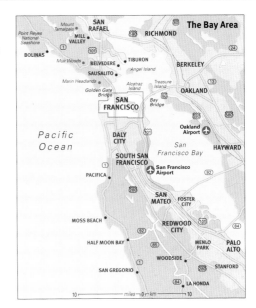

Scale of maps 1–6

0 meters — 300
0 yards — 300

Scale of maps 7–11

0 meters — 400
0 yards — 400

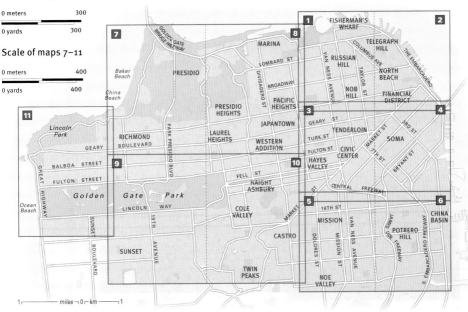

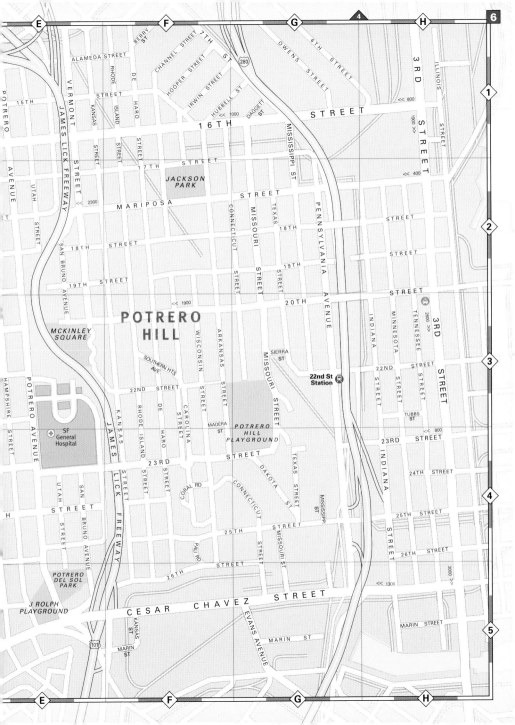

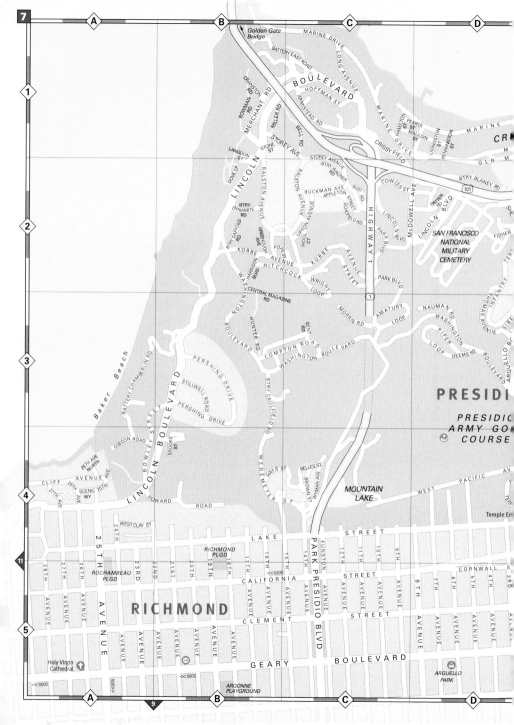

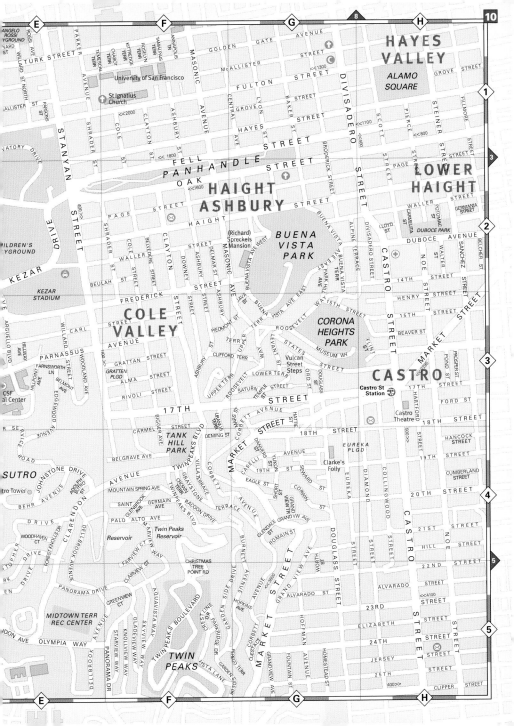

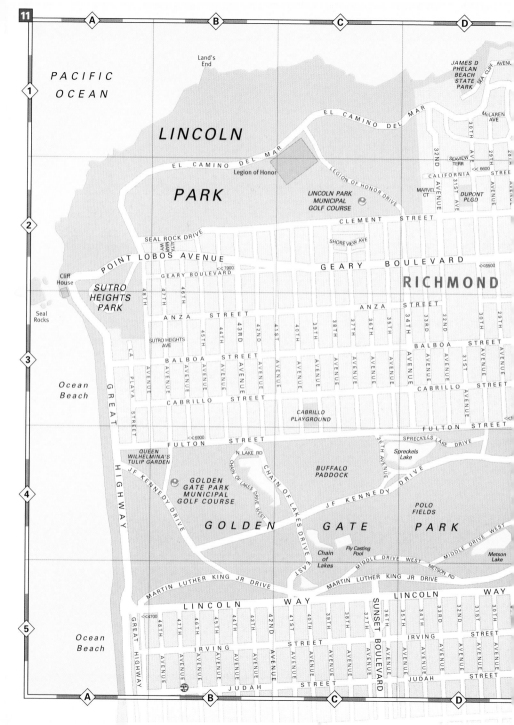

Street Finder Index

Downtown

Restaurants

For further cafés, see Havens

Chinatown

Dol Ho (p40)	$
Chinese	
Far East Café (p128)	$
Chinese	
Gold Mountain (p40)	$
Chinese	
Louie's Dim Sum (p128)	$
Chinese	
Yuet Lee Seafood (p128)	$
Chinese	

Civic Center & Tenderloin

Dottie's True Blue Café (p46)	$
Café	
Jardinière (p38)	$$$
California Cuisine	

Financial District

Aqua (p32)	$$$
French	
Rubicon (p30)	$$$
California Cuisine	
The Slanted Door (p32)	$$
Vietnamese	

Fisherman's Wharf

Eagle Café (p127)	$
Café	
Gary Danko (p32)	$$$
California Cuisine	

Jackson Square

Bix (p31)	$$$
North American	
Bocadillos (p31)	$
Tapas	
Frisson (p31)	$$
California Cuisine	
Kokkari Estiatorio (p30)	$$
Greek	
Myth (p30)	$$
California Cuisine	

Nob Hill & Polk Gulch

Pesce (p33)	$$
Fish & Seafood	
Ritz Dining Room (p32)	$$$
French	
Ritz-Carlton Terrace (p46)	$$$
California Cuisine	
Tablespoon (p33)	$$
California Cuisine	

North Beach & Russian Hill

Andrew Jaeger's House of Seafood and Jazz (p126)	$$
Fish & Seafood	
Café Jacqueline (p33)	$$
French	
Enrico's (p120)	$$
Café	
Hyde St. Seafood (p33)	$$
Fish & Seafood	
Italian French Bakery (p126)	$
Café	
Mama's (p46)	$
Café	
Mara's Italian Pastry (p127)	$
Café	
Mario's Bohemian Cigar Store (p127)	$
Café	
Moose's (p127)	$$
California Cuisine	
L'Osteria del Forno (p127)	$
Italian	
Sushi Groove (p129)	$$
Japanese	
Swenson's (p129)	$
Ice-creamery	
Washington Square Bar & Grill (p127)	$$
North American	
Zarzuela (p129)	$
Spanish	

Union Square

Café Claude (p29)	$
French	
Cortez Bar and Grill (p29)	$
Mediterranean	
Farallon (p28)	$$$
Fish & Seafood	
Fleur de Lys (p32)	$$$
French	
Masa's (p32)	$$$
French	
Postrio (p155)	$$$
North American	
Restaurant Michael Mina (p29)	$$$
California Cuisine	
Sears Fine Food (p46)	$
Café	

Shopping

Financial District

Ferry Building Marketplace (p13, p52)
Food & Drink

Jackson Square

Argentum (p53)
Antiques & Gifts

Daniel Stein (p53)
Antiques & Gifts

Dillingham & Company (p53)
Antiques & Gifts

Foster-Gwin Inc. (p53)
Antiques & Gifts

Thomas Livingston (p53)
Antiques & Gifts

North Beach & Russian Hill

101 Music (p126)
Music

AB Fits (p53, p126)
Fashion

Asia Galleries (p126)
Antiques & Gifts

Black Oak Books (p126)
Books

Brown Dirt Cowboy's (p54)
Interiors

City Lights (p53)
Books

Old Vogue (p126)
Fashion

XOX Truffles (p54)
Food & Drink

Union Square

Banana Republic (p61)
Fashion

Britex Fabrics (p55)
Fabrics

David Stephen (p55)
Fashion

De Vera (p55)
Antiques & Gifts

Diesel (p61)
Fashion

Diptyque (p55)
Antiques & Gifts

The Gap (p61)
Fashion

Gump's (p54)
Department Store

Levi's (p61)
Fashion

Macy's (p56)
Department Store

Marc Jacobs (p55)
Fashion

Neiman Marcus (p56)
Department Store

Nordstrom (p56)
Department Store

Old Navy (p61)
Fashion

Saks Fifth Avenue (p56)
Department Store

Tse (p55)
Fashion

Wilkes Bashford (p55)
Fashion

Yves Saint Laurent (p55)
Fashion

Art & Architecture

Chinatown

Chinese Historical Society of America (p128)
Museum

Civic Center

Asian Art Museum (p14, p70)
Museum

City Hall (p71)
Historic Building

Fisherman's Wharf

Aquarium of the Bay (p127)
Museum

Musée Mécanique (p127)
Museum

Nob Hill

Grace Cathedral (p71)
Religious Building

North Beach & Russian Hill

Diego Rivera Gallery (p129)
Art Gallery

Saints Peter and Paul Church (p127)
Religious Building

Telegraph Hill

Coit Tower (p14, p73)
Historic Building

Union Square

Fraenkel Gallery (p71)
Art Gallery

Gallery Paule Anglim (p71)
Art Gallery

Hang (p75)
Art Gallery

John Berggruen Gallery (p71)
Art Gallery

Modernism (p71)
Art Gallery

Stephen Wirtz Gallery (p71)
Art Gallery

Xanadu Gallery (p70)
Art Gallery

Performance

Civic Center & Tenderloin

City Arts & Lectures (p94)
Lectures

Great American Music Hall (p91)
Live Music Venue

San Francisco Ballet (p93)
Dance

San Francisco Opera (p92)
Classical Music

San Francisco Symphony (p92)
Classical Music

SF War Memorial & Performing Arts Center (pp92–3)
Combined Arts

The Warfield (p91)
Live Music Venue

Nob Hill

Empire Plush Room Cabaret (p90)
Cabaret

North Beach

Beach Blanket Babylon (p89)
Comedy

Bimbo's 365 Club (p89)
Live Music Venue

Jazz at Pearl's (p88, p126)
Jazz & Blues

Punch Line Comedy Club (p89)
Comedy

Teatro ZinZanni (p91)
Circus

Union Square & Theater District

American Conservatory Theater (p90)
Theater Company

Glide Memorial United Methodist Church (p94)
Gospel

Bars & Clubs

Chinatown

Li Po Bar (p107)
Bar

Financial District

Bubble Lounge (p106)
Bar

Irish Bank (p106)
Pub

London Wine Bar (p107)
Bar

Nob Hill & Polk Gulch

Kimo's (p114)
Bar

Tonga Room (p107)
Bar

Top of the Mark (p107)
Bar

North Beach

Buena Vista Café (p111)
Bar

Caffe Trieste (p111, p126)
Cocktail Lounge

Pier 23 (p109)
Bar

Savoy Tivoli (p126)
Bar

SF Brewing Company (p104)
Pub

Spec's (p127)
Bar

Tony Nik's (p104)
Bar

Tosca Café (p104, p127)
Bar

Vesuvio (p105)
Pub

Tenderloin

Bambuddha Lounge (p109)
Club

Rx Gallery (p108)
Gallery Bar

Union Square & Theater District

Blue Lamp (p109)
Bar

Gold Dust Lounge (p109)
Bar

Harry Denton's Starlight Room
Cocktail Lounge (p108)

The Red Room (p109)
Cocktail Lounge

Redwood Room (p109)
Cocktail Lounge

Ruby Skye (p110)
Club

Havens

Chinatown

Imperial Tea Court (p126, p138)
Teahouse

Financial District

Embarcadero Center Terrace (p138)
Hideaway

Redwood Park (p140)
Green Space

Fisherman's Wharf

Bay Cruises (p140)
Ferry

Nob Hill

Grace Cathedral (p140)
Religious Building

Huntington Park (p140)
Green Space

Nob Hill Spa (p139)
Spa

North Beach & Russian Hill

Ina Coolbrith Park (p129)
Green Space

SF Art Institute Café (p140)
Café

Telegraph Hill

Filbert Steps (p140)
Hideaway

Toujours (p56)
Lingerie

Zinc Details (p57)
Interiors

Presidio Heights
Green Apple Books (p61, p129)
Books

Art & Architecture

Marina
Exploratorium (p74)
Museum

Fort Mason Center (p73)
Mixed Media

Mexican Museum (p72)
Museum

Museo ItaloAmericano (p73)
Museum

Octagon House (p130)
Historic Building

Palace of Fine Arts (p73)
Historic Building

SFMOMA Artists Gallery (p72)
Art Gallery

Vedanta Hindu Temple (p130)
Religious Building

Pacific Heights
Thomas Reynolds
Gallery (p75)
Art Gallery

Victorian Architecture (p72)
Historic Buildings

Performance

Castro
Castro Theatre (p84, p132)
Movie Theater

Haight-Ashbury
Red Vic Movie House (p96)
Movie Theater

Marina
Magic Theatre (p94)
Theater Company

Pacific Heights & Fillmore
Audium (p94)
Theater of Sound

Boom Boom Room (p95)
Jazz & Blues

The Fillmore (p95)
Live Music Venue

Rasselas On Fillmore (p95)
Jazz & Blues

St. John Coltrane African
Orthodox Church (p94)
Jazz & Blues

Bars & Clubs

Castro
Badlands (p132)
Bar

The Bar on Castro (p114)
Bar

The Café (p114, p132)
Bar

Café du Nord (p112)
Bar

Harvey's (p114, p120)
Bar

Martuni's (p113, p134)
Bar

Haight-Ashbury
Club Deluxe (p103)
Bar

Hotel Biron (p120)
Gallery Bar

Mad Dog in the Fog (p112, p131)
Pub

Noc Noc (p131)
Bar

Orbit Room (p113)
Cocktail Lounge

Underground SF (p131)
Bar

Zam Zam (p115)
Cocktail Lounge

Hayes Valley
Fly Bar (p120)
Gallery Bar

Jade (p112)
Cocktail Lounge

Marina
CC's Pierce Street Manor (p111)
Pub

MatrixFillmore (p111, p130)
Cocktail Lounge

Perry's (p113, p130)
Bar

Havens

Cole Valley
Pharmaca (p138)
Massage

Haight-Ashbury
SF Zen Center (p141)
Meditation

Japantown
Kabuki Springs & Spa (p141)
Spa

Marina
Crissy Field (p142)
Green Space

Marina Green (p140)
Green Space

Pacific Heights
Alta Plaza Park (p140)
Green Space

International Orange
Spa (p140)
Spa

Hotels

Haight-Ashbury
Stanyan Park Hotel (p158)
Cheap

Laurel Heights
Laurel Inn (p156)
Moderate

Marina
Hotel del Sol (p157)
Cheap

Motel Capri (p156)
Cheap

Pacific Heights
Hotel Drisco (p158)
Moderate

Hotel Majestic (p156)
Cheap

Jackson Court (p158)
Moderate

Western Addition
Archbishop's Mansion (p158)
Moderate

South

Restaurants

Mission
Delfina (p44) $
Italian

El Nuevo Fruitlandia (p134) $
Puerto Rican

Foreign Cinema (p44) $
California Cuisine

Levende Lounge (p43) $
International/Fusion

Luna Park (p42, p134) $
International/Fusion

La Rondalla (p41) $
Mexican

Tartine Bakery (p46) $
Café

Ti Couz (p42, p134) $
French

Noe Valley
Hamano Sushi (p44) $$
Japanese

Savor (p133) $
French

Le Zinc French Bistro (p133) $$
French

Potrero Hill
Aperto (p133) $
Italian

Baraka (p43) $$
Moroccan

Art & Architecture

Golden Gate Park

The Beach Chalet (p82)
Historic Building

de Young Museum (p15, p79)
Museum

Laurel Heights

Neptune Society Columbarium (p79)
Religious Building

Lincoln Park

Legion of Honor (pp80–81)
Museum

Sunset

The Canvas (p75, p120)
Art Gallery

Bars & Clubs

Richmond

Plough and Stars (p122, p129)
Pub

Trad'r Sam's (p122)
Bar

Havens

Golden Gate Park

Beach Chalet (p145)
Restaurant

Conservatory of Flowers (p145)
Green Space

Golden Gate Park (p13, pp144–5)
Green Space

Japanese Tea Garden (p145)
Teahouse

National AIDS Memorial Grove (p145)
Green Space

Park Chalet (p145)
Café

SF Botanical Garden (p145)
Green Space

Sunset

Sunset Sauna & Massage (p138)
Spa

Hotels

Ocean Beach

Seal Rock Inn (p159)
Cheap

East Bay

Cafés & Restaurants

Berkeley

Blondie's Pizza (p135) $
Pizza

César (p47) $
Tapas

Chez Panisse (p46) $$–$$$
California Cuisine

French Hotel Café (p47) $
Café

Juice Bar Collective (p47) $
Café

Masse's Pastries (p47) $
Café

Oakland

A Côté (p47, p135) $$
French

Nan Yang (p135) $$
Burmese

Oliveto (p135) $$
Italian

Zachary's Chicago Pizza (p46) $
Pizza

Shopping

Berkeley

Annapurna (p135)
Novelty

Cheese Board Collective (p47)
Food & Drink

Cody's Books (p135)
Books

The Gardener (p65)
Interiors

George (p64)
Pets Accessories

Margaret O'Leary (p65)
Fashion

Moe's (p135)
Books

Peet's Coffee & Tea (p47)
East Bay/Berkeley

Oakland

Rockridge Market Hall (p135)
Food & Drink

Rockridge Rags (p135)
Thrift Store

Tail of the Yak (p65)
Antiques & Gifts

Art & Architecture

Berkeley

Berkeley Art Museum (p82)
Museum

Oakland

Chapel of the Chimes (p73)
Religious Building

Mountain View Cemetery (p83)
Religious Building

Paramount Theatre (p82)
Historic Building

Performance

Berkeley

Berkeley Repertory (p99)
Theater Company

Cal Performances (p98)
Combined Arts

Shotgun Players (p99)
Theater Company

Oakland

The Golden State Warriors (p96)
Sports

Oakland A's (p96)
Sports

Oakland Raiders (p96)
Sports

Parkway Speakeasy Theater (p99)
Movie Theater

Yoshi's (p99)
Jazz & Blues

Bars & Clubs

Berkeley

Albatross (p123)
Pub

Blake's (p135)
Bar

Jupiter (p123)
Pub

Oakland

The Alley (p123)
Bar

Heinold's First and Last Chance Saloon (p123)
Bar

Kingman's Lucky Lounge (p123)
Bar

Marin County

Restaurants

Sam's Anchor Café (p47) $
Fish & Seafood

Sushi Ran (p47) $$$
Japanese

Havens

Marin Headlands (p141)
Green Space

Mount Tamalpais (p141)
Green Space

Muir Woods (p141)
Green Space

Point Reyes National Seashore (p141)
Green Space

Restaurants

Further restaurants and cafés are listed under Havens

Cafés

Caffè Museo (p79) $
South/SoMa

de Young Café (p79) $
West/Golden Gate Park

Dottie's True Blue Café (p40) $
Downtown/Tenderloin

Eagle Café (p127) $
Downtown/Fisherman's Wharf

Enrico's (p126) $
Downtown/North Beach

French Hotel Café (p47) $
East Bay/Berkeley

Imperial Tea Court (p126) $
Downtown/North Beach

Italian French Bakery (p126) $
Downtown/North Beach

Juice Bar Collective (p47) $
East Bay/Berkeley

Kate's Kitchen (p131) $
North & Central/Haight-Ashbury

Legion of Honor Café (p79) $
West/Lincoln Park

Mama's (p46) $
Downtown/North Beach

Mara's Italian Pastry (p127) $
Downtown/North Beach

Mario's Bohemian $
Cigar Store (p127)
Downtown/North Beach

Masse's Pastries (p47) $
East Bay/Berkeley

Sears Fine Food (p46) $
Downtown/Union Square

Squat and Gobble $
Café (p131)
North & Central/Haight-Ashbury

Swenson's (p129) $
Downtown/Russian Hill

Tartine Bakery (p46) $
South/Mission

Burmese

Burma Superstar (p129) $
North & Central/Presidio

Nan Yang (p135) $$
East Bay/Oakland

California Cuisine

Chez Panisse (p46) $$–$$$
East Bay/Berkeley

Foreign Cinema (p44) $$
South/Mission

Frisson (p31) $$
Downtown/Jackson Square

Gary Danko (p32) $$$
Downtown/Fisherman's Wharf

Jardinière (p38) $$$
Downtown/Civic Center

Mecca (p39, p132) $$
North & Central/Castro

Moose's (p127) $$
Downtown/North Beach

Myth (p30) $$
Downtown/Jackson Square

Nectar Wine Lounge (p37) $$
North & Central/Marina

Oola (p40) $$
South/SoMa

Restaurant Michael $$$
Mina (p29)
Downtown/Union Square

Ritz-Carlton Terrace (p46) $$$
Downtown/Nob Hill

RNM Restaurant (p38) $$
North & Central/Lower Haight

Rubicon (p30) $$$
Downtown/Financial District

Slow Club (p42) $
South/Potrero Hill

Tablespoon (p33) $$
Downtown/Polk Gulch

Zuni Café (p38) $$
North & Central/Lower Haight

Chinese

Dol Ho (p40) $
Downtown/Chinatown

Far East Café (p128) $
Downtown/Chinatown

Gold Mountain (p40) $
Downtown/Chinatown

Gourmet Carousel (p37) $
North & Central/Pacific Heights

Louie's Dim Sum (p128) $
Downtown/Chinatown

Ton Kiang (p40) $
West/Richmond

Yank Sing (p40) $
South/SoMa

Yuet Lee Seafood (p128) $
Downtown/Chinatown

Ethiopian

Axum Café (p131) $
North & Central/Haight-Ashbury

Fish & Seafood

Andrew Jaeger's House of $$
Seafood and Jazz (p126)
Downtown/North Beach

Catch (p132) $$
North & Central/Castro

Farallon (p28) $$$
Downtown/Union Square

Hyde St. Seafood (p33) $$
Downtown/Russian Hill

Pesce (p33) $$
Downtown/Polk Gulch

Sam's Anchor Café (p47) $
Marin County/Tiburon

French

A Côté (p47, p135) $$
East Bay/Oakland

Aqua (p32) $$$
Downtown/Financial District

Café Claude (p29) $
Downtown/Union Square

Café Jacqueline (p33) $$
Downtown/North Beach

Chez Papa Bistrot (p43) $$
South/Potrero Hill

Clementine (p129) $
North & Central/Presidio

Fifth Floor (p32) $$$
South/SoMa

Fleur de Lys (p32) $$$
Downtown/Union Square

Masa's (p32) $$$
Downtown/Union Square

Ritz Dining Room (p32) $$$
Downtown/Nob Hill

Savor (p133) $
South/Noe Valley

Ti Couz (p42, p134) $
South/Mission

Le Zinc French Bistro (p133) $$
South/Noe Valley

Greek

Kokkari Estiatorio (p30) $$
Downtown/Jackson Square

International/Fusion

Ame (p41) $$$
South/SoMa

Levende Lounge (p43) $
South/Mission

Lime (p37) $
North & Central/Castro

Luna Park (p42, p134) $
South/Mission

Italian

A16 (p36) $$
North & Central/Marina

Aperto (p133) $
South/Potrero Hill

Delfina (p44) $
South/Mission

Oliveto (p135) $$
East Bay/Oakland

L'Osteria del Forno (p127) $
Downtown/North Beach

Quince (p37) $$
North & Central/Pacific Heights

Japanese

Hamano Sushi (p44) $$
South/Noe Valley

Sushi Groove (p129) $$
Downtown/Russian Hill

Sushi Ran (p47) $$$
Marin County/Sausalito

Mediterranean

Cortez Bar and Grill (p29) $
Downtown/Union Square

La Méditerranée (p37) $
North & Central/Fillmore

Mexican

La Rondalla (p41) $
South/Mission

Moroccan

Baraka (p43) $$
South/Potrero Hill

North American

Balboa Café (p37) $$
North & Central/Cow Hollow

Beach Chalet (p145) $
West/Golden Gate Park

Bix (p31) $$$
Downtown/Jackson Square

Chow (p39) $
North & Central/Castro

Cliff House Bistro (p45) $$
West/Ocean Beach

Mel's Drive-In (p130) $
North & Central/Marina

Postrio (p155) $$$
Downtown/Union Square

Sutro's (p45) $$$
West/Ocean Beach

Town Hall (p40) $$
South/SoMa

Washington Square Bar & Grill (p127) $$
Downtown/North Beach

Pan-Asian

AsiaSF (p40) $$
South/SoMa

Café Asia (p79) $
Downtown/Civic Center

Pizza

Blondie's Pizza (p135) $
East Bay/Berkeley

Zachary's Chicago Pizza (p46) $
East Bay/Oakland

Puerto Rican

El Nuevo Fruitlandia (p134) $
South/Mission

Spanish

Zarzuela (p129) $
Downtown/Russian Hill

Steakhouses

Acme Chophouse (p40) $$
South/South Beach

Izzy's Steak and Chop House (p130) $$
North & Central/Marina

Tapas

Bocadillos (p31) $
Downtown/Jackson Square

César (p47) $
East Bay/Berkeley

Thai

Thep Phanom (p131) $
North & Central/Haight-Ashbury

Vegetarian

Greens (p36) $
North & Central/Marina

Vietnamese

The Slanted Door (p32) $$
Downtown/Financial District

Shopping

Antiques & Gifts

Argentum (p53)
Downtown/Jackson Square

Asia Galleries (p126)
Downtown/North Beach

Bell'occhio (p63)
North & Central/Lower Haight

Daniel Stein (p53)
Downtown/Jackson Square

De Vera (p55)
Downtown/Union Square

Dillingham & Company (p53)
Downtown/Jackson Square

Diptyque (p55)
Downtown/Union Square

Foster-Gwin Inc. (p53)
Downtown/Jackson Square

Little Tibet (p130)
North & Central/Marina

Tail of the Yak (p65)
East Bay/Oakland

Thomas Livingston (p53)
Downtown/Jackson Square

Books

Black Oak Books (p126)
Downtown/North Beach

Books Inc. (p130)
North & Central/Marina

City Lights (p53)
Downtown/North Beach

Cody's Books (p135)
East Bay/Berkeley

Comix Experience (p131)
North & Central/Haight-Ashbury

Green Apple Books (p61, p129)
North & Central/Presidio

Moe's (p135)
East Bay/Berkeley

Department Stores

Gump's (p54)
Downtown/Union Square

Macy's (p56)
Downtown/Union Square

Neiman Marcus (p56)
Downtown/Union Square

Nordstrom (p56)
Downtown/Union Square

Saks Fifth Avenue (p56)
Downtown/Union Square

Entertainment

Metreon (p62)
South/SoMa

Fabrics

Britex Fabrics (p55)
Downtown/Union Square

Fair Trade

Global Exchange (p133)
South/Noe Valley

Fashion

AB Fits (p53, p126)
Downtown/North Beach

Azalea (p58)
North & Central/Hayes Valley

Banana Republic (p61)
Downtown/Union Square

David Stephen (p55)
Downtown/Union Square

Diesel (p61)
Downtown/Union Square

Divine Girls (p60)
North & Central/Pacific Heights

The Gap (p61)
Downtown/Union Square

Levi's (p61)
Downtown/Union Square

Marc Jacobs (p55)
Downtown/Union Square

Margaret O'Leary (p65)
East Bay/Berkeley

Mrs. Dewson's Hats (p57)
North & Central/Pacific Heights

Nida (p58)
North & Central/Hayes Valley

Index by Type

For the very latest on San Francisco go to »» www.realcity.dk.com

Coit Tower (p14, p73)
Downtown/Telegraph Hill

Octagon House (p130)
North & Central/Marina

Palace of Fine Arts (p73)
North & Central/Marina

Paramount Theatre (p82)
East Bay/Oakland

Victorian Architecture (p72)
North & Central/Pacific Heights

Mixed Media

Fort Mason Center (p73)
North & Central/Marina

New Langton Arts (p75)
South/SoMa

Yerba Buena Center for the
Arts (p74)
South/SoMa

Mural Art

Precita Eyes Mural Arts (p75)
South/Mission

Women's Building (p134)
South/Mission

Museums

Asian Art Museum (p14, p70)
Downtown/Civic Center

Berkeley Art Museum (p82)
East Bay/Berkeley

Cartoon Art Museum (p74)
South/SoMa

Chinese Historical Society of
America (p128)
Downtown/Chinatown

de Young Museum (p15, p79)
West/Golden Gate Park

Exploratorium (p74)
North & Central/Marina

Legion of Honor (pp80–81)
West/Lincoln Park

Musée Mécanique (p127)
Downtown/North Beach

Museo ItaloAmericano (p73)
North & Central/Marina

Museum of Craft
and Folk Art (p74)
South/SoMa

San Francisco Museum of
Modern Art (p78)
South/SoMa

Religious Buildings

Chapel of the Chimes (p83)
East Bay/Oakland

Grace Cathedral (p59)
Downtown/Nob Hill

Memorial Church (p78)
South/Stanford

Mission Dolores (p75, p134)
South/Mission

Mountain View Cemetery (p71)
East Bay/Oakland

Neptune Society
Columbarium (p79)
West/Laurel Heights

Saints Peter and Paul
Church (p127)
Downtown/North Beach

Tin How Temple (p70)
Downtown/Chinatown

Vedanta Hindu Temple (p130)
North & Central/Marina

Performance

Cabaret

Empire Plush Room
Cabaret (p90)
Downtown/Nob Hill

Circus

Teatro ZinZanni (p91)
Downtown/North Beach

Classical Music

San Francisco Opera (p92)
Downtown/Civic Center

San Francisco
Performances (p88)
Various venues

San Francisco Symphony (p92)
Downtown/Civic Center

Combined Arts

Cal Performances (p98)
East Bay/Berkeley

Intersection for the Arts (p97)
South/Mission

The Marsh (p97)
South/Mission

SF War Memorial & Performing
Arts Center (pp92–3)
Downtown/Civic Center

Yerba Buena Center
for the Arts (p97)
South/SoMa

Comedy

Beach Blanket Babylon (p89)
Downtown/North Beach

Killing My Lobster (p90)
Various venues

Punch Line Comedy Club (p89)
Downtown/North Beach

Dance

Joe Goode Performance
Group (p90)
Various venues

LINES Ballet (p90)
Various venues

Robert Moses' Kin (p90)
Various venues

San Francisco Ballet (p93)
Downtown/Civic Center

Smuin Ballet (p90)
Various venues

Jazz & Blues

Boom Boom Room (p95)
North & Central/Fillmore

Jazz at Pearl's (p88, p127)
Downtown/North Beach

Rasselas On Fillmore (p95)
North & Central/Fillmore

St. John Coltrane African
Orthodox Church (p94)
North & Central/Fillmore

Yoshi's (p99)
East Bay/Oakland

Gospel

Glide United Memorial
Methodist Church (p94)
Downtown/Union Square

Lectures

City Arts & Lectures (p94)
Downtown/Civic Center

Live Music Venues

Bimbo's 365 Club (p89)
Downtown/North Beach

The Fillmore (p89)
North & Central/Fillmore

Great American Music
Hall (p91)
Downtown/Tenderloin

The Warfield (p91)
Downtown/Tenderloin

Movie Theaters

Castro Theatre (p96)
North & Central/Castro

Parkway Speakeasy
Theater (p99)
East Bay/Oakland

Red Vic Movie House (p96)
North & Central/Haight-Ashbury

Sports

AT&T Park (p97)
South/South Beach

The Golden State
Warriors (p96)
East Bay/Oakland

Oakland A's (p96)
East Bay/Oakland

The Raiders (p96)
East Bay/Oakland

Index by Type

Performance

Theater Companies

42nd Street Moon (p90)
Various venues

American Conservatory Theater (p90)
Downtown/Theater District

Berkeley Repertory (p99)
East Bay/Berkeley

Encore Theatre Company (p90)
Various venues

Magic Theatre (p94)
North & Central/Marina

Shotgun Players (p99)
East Bay/Berkeley

Theatre Rhinoceros (p96)
South/Mission

Theater of Sound

Audium (p94)
North & Central/Pacific Heights

Bars & Clubs

Ballroom

Metronome Dance Center (p119)
South/Potrero Hill

Bars

The Alley (p119)
East Bay/Oakland

Badlands (p132)
North & Central/Castro

Balboa Café (p37)
North & Central/Cow Hollow

The Bar on Castro (p114)
North & Central/Castro

Blake's (p135)
East Bay/Berkeley

Blue Lamp (p109)
Downtown/Theater District

Bottom of the Hill (p120, p133)
South/Potrero Hill

Bruno's (p134)
South/Mission

Bubble Lounge (p106)
Downtown/Financial District

Buena Vista Café (p111)
Downtown/North Beach

Buzz 9 (p118)
South/SoMa

The Café (p114, p132)
North & Central/Castro

Café du Nord (p112)
North & Central/Castro

Club Deluxe (p115)
North & Central/Haight-Ashbury

Elbo Room (p120)
South/Mission

G-Bar (p144)
North & Central/Pacific Heights

Gold Dust Lounge (p109)
Downtown/Union Square

Harvey's (p114, p132)
North & Central/Castro

Heinold's First and Last Chance Saloon (p123)
East Bay/Oakland

Kimo's (p114)
Downtown/Polk Gulch

Kingman's Lucky Lounge (p123)
East Bay/Oakland

Levende (p43)
South/Mission

Lime (p39)
North & Central/Castro

Li Po Bar (p107)
Downtown/Chinatown

London Wine Bar (p107)
Downtown/Financial District

Make-Out Room (p119)
South/Mission

Martuni's (p113, p134)
North & Central/Castro

Noc Noc (p131)
North & Central/Haight-Ashbury

Perry's (p113, p130)
North & Central/Cow Hollow

Phone Booth (p114)
South/Mission

Pier 23 (p109)
Downtown/North Beach

The Saloon (p109, p126)
Downtown/North Beach

Savoy Tivoli (p126)
Downtown/North Beach

Spec's (p127)
Downtown/North Beach

Tonga Room (p107)
Downtown/Nob Hill

Tony Nik's (p104)
Downtown/North Beach

Underground SF (p131)
North & Central/Haight-Ashbury

Top of the Mark (p107)
Downtown/Nob Hill

Tosca Café (p104, p127)
Downtown/North Beach

Trad'r Sam's (p122)
West/Richmond

W Café (p158)
South/SoMa

Wild Side West (p121)
South/Bernal Heights

Clubs

12 Galaxies (p119)
South/Mission

Duplex (p119)
South/SoMa

El Rio (p122)
South/Mission

The EndUp (p112)
South/SoMa

Mezzanine (p118)
South/SoMa

Ruby Skye (p110)
Downtown/Union Square

The Stud (p114)
South/SoMa

Cocktail Lounges

Caffe Trieste (p111, p126)
Downtown/North Beach

Harry Denton's Starlight Room (p108)
Downtown/Union Square

Jade (p112)
North & Central/Hayes Valley

MatrixFillmore (p111, p130)
North & Central/Cow Hollow

Orbit Room (p113)
North & Central/Lower Haight

The Red Room (p109)
Downtown/Union Square

Redwood Room (p109)
Downtown/Union Square

Zam Zam (p115)
North & Central/Haight-Ashbury

Gallery Bars

The Canvas (p75, p120)
West/Sunset

Fly Bar (p120)
North & Central/Hayes Valley

Hotel Biron (p120)
North & Central/Lower Haight

Rx Gallery (p120)
Downtown/Tenderloin

Pubs

Albatross (p123)
East Bay/Berkeley

CC's Pierce Street Manor (p111)
North & Central/Marina

Irish Bank (p106)
Downtown/Financial District

Jupiter (p123)
East Bay/Berkeley

Mad Dog in the Fog (p112, p131)
North & Central/Haight-Ashbury

The Plough and Stars (p122, p131)
West/Richmond

SF Brewing Company (p104)
Downtown/North Beach

Thirsty Bear (p118)
South/SoMa

Vesuvio (p105)
Downtown/North Beach

Zeitgeist (p121)
South/Mission

Havens

Cafés and Teahouses

Imperial Tea Court (p138)
Downtown/Chinatown

Japanese Tea Garden (p145)
West/Golden Gate Park

Park Chalet (p145)
West/Golden Gate Park

SF Art Institute Café (p140)
Downtown/Russian Hill

Ferry Trips

Bay Cruises (p138)
Downtown/Fisherman's Wharf

Green Spaces

Alta Plaza Park (p140)
North & Central/Pacific Heights

Conservatory of Flowers (p145)
West/Golden Gate Park

Crissy Field (p142)
North & Central/Marina

Golden Gate Park (p13, pp144–5)
West/Golden Gate Park

Huntington Park (p140)
Downtown/Nob Hill

Ina Coolbrith Park (p129)
Downtown/Russian Hill

Marina Green (p140)
North & Central/Marina

Marin Headlands (p141)
Marin County

Mount Tamalpais (p141)
Marin County

Muir Woods (p141)
Marin County

National AIDS Memorial Grove (p145)
West/Golden Gate Park

Point Reyes National Seashore (p141)
Marin County

Redwood Park (p134)
Downtown/Financial District

SF Botanical Garden (p145)
West/Golden Gate Park

Yerba Buena Gardens (p143)
South/SoMa

Hideaways

Embarcadero Center Terrace (p138)
Downtown/Financial District

Filbert Steps (p140)
Downtown/Telegraph Hill

Meditation

SF Zen Center (p141)
North & Central/Lower Haight

Religious Building

Grace Cathedral (p140)
Downtown/Nob Hill

Restaurant

Beach Chalet (p145)
West/Golden Gate Park

Spas and Massage

Elephant Pharmacy (p138)
East Bay/Berkeley

International Orange Spa (p140)
North & Central/Pacific Heights

Kabuki Springs & Spa (p141)
North & Central/Japantown

Nob Hill Spa (p139)
Downtown/Nob Hill

Pharmaca (p138)
North & Central/Cole Valley

Sunset Sauna & Massage (p138)
West/Sunset

Hotels

Expensive

Campton Place (p153)
Downtown/Union Square

Four Seasons (p152)
Downtown/Financial District

Hotel Vitale (p159)
South/SoMa

Huntington Hotel (p151)
Downtown/Nob Hill

Omni San Francisco (p150)
Downtown/Financial District

Ritz-Carlton (p152)
Downtown/Nob Hill

Park Hyatt (p150)
Downtown/Financial District

St. Regis San Francisco (p158)
South/SoMa

W San Francisco (p158)
South/SoMa

Moderate

Archbishop's Mansion (p158)
North & Central/Western Add.

Fairmont San Francisco (p153)
Downtown/Nob Hill

Harbor Court Hotel (p159)
South/SoMa

Hotel Adagio (p155)
Downtown/Theater District

Hotel Bohème (p156)
Downtown/North Beach

Hotel Drisco (p158)
North & Central/Pacific Heights

Hotel Griffon (p159)
South/SoMa

Hotel Monaco (p150)
Downtown/Theater District

Hotel Triton (p154)
Downtown/Union Square

InterContinental Mark Hopkins (p153)
Downtown/Nob Hill

Jackson Court (p158)
North & Central/Pacific Heights

Laurel Inn (p156)
North & Central/Laurel Heights

Nob Hill Lambourne (p152)
Downtown/Nob Hill

Palace Hotel (p153)
South/SoMa

Prescott Hotel (p155)
Downtown/Union Square

Sir Francis Drake (p153)
Downtown/Union Square

Washington Square Inn (p158)
Downtown/North Beach

Westin St. Francis (p153)
Downtown/Union Square

Cheap

Commodore Hotel (p155)
Downtown/Union Square

Hotel Majestic (p156)
North & Central/Pacific Heights

Hotel Rex (p154)
Downtown/Union Square

Hotel del Sol (p157)
North & Central/Marina

Motel Capri (p156)
North & Central/Marina

Phoenix Hotel (p154)
Downtown/Tenderloin

Seal Rock Inn (p159)
West/Ocean Beach

Stanyan Park Hotel (p158)
North & Central/Haight-Ashbury

General Index

General Index

Acknowledgments

Published by DK

Publishing Managers Jane Ewart and Scarlett O'Hara

Senior Editor Christine Stroyan

Senior Designer Paul Jackson

Editor Jenny Finch

Assistant Editor Jenny Piening

Designer Bernhard Wolf Koppmeyer

Picture Research Gina Risso

Proofreader Gary Werner

Indexer Helen Peters

Website Editor Gouri Banerji

Cartographic Editor Casper Morris

DTP Designers Jason Little and Natasha Lu

Production Controller Shane Higgins

Fact Checker Susan Charles Bush

Revisions Departure Lounge LLP

PHOTOGRAPHY PERMISSIONS

Dorling Kindersley would like to thank all the museums, hotels, restaurants, bars, clubs, shops, galleries and other sights for their assistance and kind permission to photograph at their establishments. The publishers are also grateful to Martin Travers for giving permission to use the image of his Balmy Alley mural *A New Day* (p75 top right).

Placement Key: tr = top right; c = centre; cl = centre left; cla = centre left above; cra = centre right above; cr = centre right; crb = centre right below; bl = bottom left; br = bottom right

The publishers would like to thank the following companies and picture libraries for permission to reproduce their photographs:

ALAMY IMAGES: Art Kowalky 1.

AME: Joe Fletcher 41br.

BLUE & GOLD FLEET: 138cr.

CANTOR ARTS CENTER: courtesy of Betty Cantor Jackson 78cr.

DELFINA: 44bl.

DIVINE GIRLS: Lindsay Kelley 60bl.

DUPLEX: 119tr.

FOUR SEASONS HOTEL: 152br.

GETTY IMAGES: Peter Gridley/Taxi 6-7.

HOTEL MAJESTIC: 156cla.

INTERNATIONAL ORANGE SPA: 140crb.

MAGIC THEATRE: 94cla.

MEMORIAL CHURCH: 78bl.

MUSEUM OF CRAFT & FOLK ART: 74cra.

PARAMOUNT THEATRE: 82bl.

SFCVB: 15cr; Phil Coblentz 12br; Bob Ecker 13c; Jerry Lee Hayes 15tr.

SUMBODY: 56tr.

SUNHEE MOON: 64tr.

TEATRO ZINZANNI: 91bl.

TOWN HALL: 40tl.

DE YOUNG MUSEUM: 15br, 79tr.

Full Page Picture Captions: Arion Press: 2–3; Tosca Café: 8–9; Jardinière 24–5; Frisson: 34–5, 100–101; Shop, Hayes Street: 48–9; Asian Art Museum: 66–7; Xanadu Gallery: 76–7; Fillmore District: 84–5; SoMa Club: 116–17; Cable Car, Russian Hill: 124–5; Embarcadero Center Terrace: 136–7; Omni San Francisco: 146–7

Jacket Images

Front and Spine: ALAMY IMAGES: Art Kowalsky.

Back: DK IMAGES: all.

Special Editions of DK Travel Guides

San Francisco Tranport Map

Bart Lines

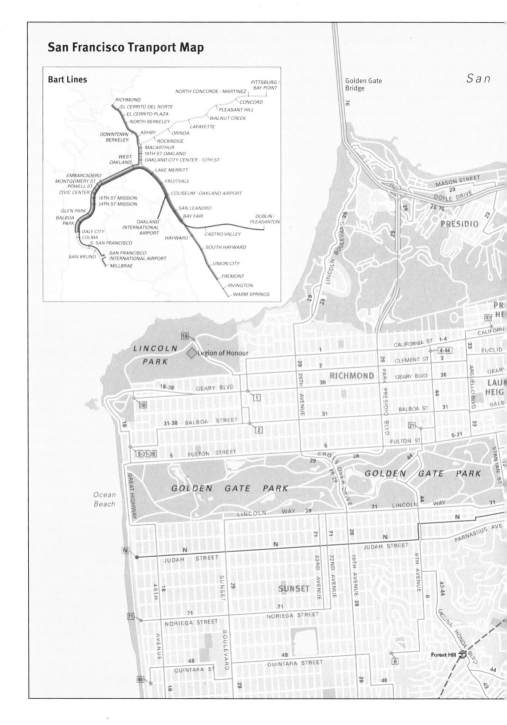

PITTSBURG / BAY POINT
NORTH CONCORDE / MARTINEZ
CONCORD
PLEASANT HILL
WALNUT CREEK
RICHMOND
EL CERRITO DEL NORTE
EL CERRITO PLAZA
NORTH BERKELEY
LAFAYETTE
DOWNTOWN BERKELEY
ASHBY
ORINDA
ROCKRIDGE
MACARTHUR
19TH ST OAKLAND
WEST OAKLAND
OAKLAND CITY CENTER · 12TH ST
LAKE MERRITT
EMBARCADERO
MONTGOMERY ST
POWELL ST
CIVIC CENTER
FRUITVALE
COLISEUM / OAKLAND AIRPORT
16TH ST MISSION
24TH ST MISSION
SAN LEANDRO
GLEN PARK
BALBOA PARK
BAY FAIR
DUBLIN / PLEASANTON
DALY CITY
COLMA
OAKLAND INTERNATIONAL AIRPORT
CASTRO VALLEY
S. SAN FRANCISCO
HAYWARD
SAN BRUNO
SAN FRANCISCO INTERNATIONAL AIRPORT
SOUTH HAYWARD
MILLBRAE
UNION CITY
FREMONT
IRVINGTON
WARM SPRINGS

Golden Gate Bridge

San

MASON STREET
DOYLE DRIVE

PRESIDIO

LINCOLN BOULEVARD

PR HE

LINCOLN PARK

Legion of Honour

CALIFORNIA ST 1-4
CLEMENT ST
RICHMOND
GEARY BLVD
EUCLID
GEAR
LAU HEIG
BALB

GEARY BLVD
18-38
BALBOA ST

31-38 BALBOA STREET

BALBOA STREET

FULTON ST
5-21

5-31-38 5 FULTON STREET

CROSS OVER DRIVE

GOLDEN GATE PARK

GOLDEN GATE PARK

Ocean Beach

GREAT HIGHWAY

LINCOLN WAY

LINCOLN WAY

PARNASSUS AVE

JUDAH STREET

JUDAH STREET

SUNSET

SUNSET BOULEVARD

NORIEGA STREET

NORIEGA STREET

Forest Hill

QUINTARA ST

QUINTARA STREET

AVENUE

PRESIDIO

PARK PRESIDIO BLVD

ARGUELLO BLVD

STANYAN ST

LAGUNA HONDA BLVD